The Spaces In Between

A Memoir

Caroline Jones

Constable • London

CONSTABLE

Some names and details have been changed to protect the privacy of others.

First published in Great Britain in 2016 by Constable
This paperback edition published in 2017

1 3 5 7 9 10 8 6 4 2

Copyright © Caroline Jones, 2016

All internal images provided by the Jones family

The moral right of the author has been asserted.

A CIP catalogue record for this book
is available from the British Library.

ISBN 978-1-47212-165-3

Typeset in ITC New Baskerville by SX Composing DTP, Rayleigh, Essex
Printed and bound in Great Britain by Clays Ltd, St Ives PLC

Papers used by Constable are from well-managed forests and
other responsible resources.

MIX
Paper from
responsible sources
FSC® C104740

Constable
An imprint of
Little, Brown Book Group
Carmelite House
50 Victoria Embankment
London EC4Y 0DZ

An Hachette UK Company
www.hachette.co.uk

www.littlebrown.co.uk

*Every effort has been made to obtain the necessary permissions with reference to copyright
material, both illustrative and quoted. We apologise for any omissions in this respect and
will be pleased to make the appropriate acknowledgements in any future edition.*

For my mother and father,
whose joy for life took us all on an incredible journey.

In our Kenyan garden, 1981.

Contents

PART I:
ENGLAND
2006

Me on the right. Four years old. Lesotho, 1978.

One

A Tuesday afternoon in London. March 2006.
Thirty-one years old

I'm at my desk at the BBC, the unwelcome features of Fran, my director, foremost in my field of vision. The open-plan office balloons outwards from her head, photocopiers whirring, ergonomic desk chairs on worn carpets, a yellowed sign dangling from the ceiling, and somewhere on the edge of things the pink cardigan of the production secretary bending over a printer, tugging at a mangled piece of paper.

I have hardly left my desk today, working at my screen, on the phone, sifting through piles of unread documents and newspaper cuttings and website search results, trying to find a way out of the bog in which we find ourselves mired. My boss is furious that once again access we have requested from the organisers of London's Olympic Games has been denied.

Fran glares at me. 'What about the newts?' she says.

I explain that I have had no confirmation of the story I read in one of the many pieces of propaganda released by the organisers that a colony of rare newts is, at this very moment, being rescued from the Olympic Park and relocated to a nearby nature park ahead of demolition work. This would be a colourful story to follow for obvious reasons – the juxtaposition of the big and the small, and a typically British endeavour, just the kind of thing the BBC loves. I can picture the scene – conservation officers bent over in the long grass of a derelict East London lot, encouraging reluctant newts from their habitat, while behind them voracious bulldozers demolish East End buildings, laying bare the earth to make way for the Olympic Stadium.

My efforts to verify the story, though, have failed. It's like a maze – like a nightmarish Borges story I read at university of a maze within a maze – trying to get any straight answers from the Olympics' organisers, and as the local London boroughs have signed a confidentiality agreement, I cannot turn to them for information either. They have now physically cordoned off the area so we can't even get in to see for ourselves unless they grant us passes, which they do stingily and after long delays.

'I'll try the press officer again,' I say. I pick up the phone, dial her number. It goes through to voicemail. 'Emma, it's Caroline Jones here from the BBC. Just wondering if you or someone else could get back to me on the newts story. Today, if possible. Thanks.'

'I can't see how they don't understand that this would be a great bit of PR for them.' Fran's face is red. 'By the time they bother to get back to us they'll have cleared out all the fucking newts from the park and we'll have missed the whole thing. Again!'

I can't help thinking this is personal. Is there something I'm not doing that means we never seem to make progress on this project? I look down at the pile of papers on my desk. Perhaps I've missed something. I picture the newt relocation van, its engine revving, as the last of the great crested newts is lifted from the long grass and held triumphantly aloft. The doors slam and the van disappears in a cloud of dust down a long road to a newt paradise outside the designated Olympic area. I know Fran is thinking something similar. I shake my head. I frown and sigh audibly. It's good for my boss to see my frustration, to know that I do care about this as much as she does, but at the same time it's my job to remain resourceful and positive.

'Do you think it would be a good idea to contact Adrian again and let him know we're not getting the help we need from his team?' I suggest. 'If we're not getting access to this, of all stories, then I think it's unlikely they'll even consider any of the other stories we want to follow.'

'Yes,' she softens. 'Will you send him an email and make sure you copy me.'

Then she stands up and leaves the open-plan office. I watch her striped cashmere sweater disappear through the swing doors at one end. I know that sweater, its softness, the way it fits her; it has reappeared over the time we've been working together on various projects, all of them successful until now. The swing doors slow and still. I know my director well, within this context at least, and we are friends, in a limited kind of way, within the boundaries of work. I'm useful to her and she is useful to me too. And I like working with her, most of the time. Our film about Christine, a mother with early-onset Alzheimer's, has just transmitted and has been nominated for a prestigious television award. It ends with Christine swimming in the sea at Southwold, where she finally finds a freedom of sorts. When we first met her she had sworn she would one day swim out into this sea, a beautiful spot off a sandy stretch of Suffolk, and never return. But by the time we got there, at the end of a year of filming, she had forgotten that that was what she had intended to do, and we watched her swim happily back to shore.

I look away from the motionless swing doors to the clock on the wall. It's only 4.30 p.m. I look down at my list of things to do and feel a heavy reluctance to tackle any of it. The project feels doomed. And lurking somewhere in my dark subconscious is the feeling that I should never have agreed to this project, because, fundamentally, I am simply not interested in the London Olympics. But I'm on it, and I'm on it for several more months.

I brush imaginary dust off the pile of papers on my desk. Maybe it *is* my fault that it isn't working. Perhaps somebody else would be doing a better job of this. Laura, for example. Laura was on the project before me. She was professional, calm, controlled, with an absolute dedication to detail. When she was on the project she kept a paper cup on the desk on which she had written 'Sticky Bun', in which the team would put coins for teas and coffees.

On second thoughts, Laura was perhaps lacking in the broader, creative picture; and the earthier human touch that Fran likes. Laura was wise to move on. The cup is still there, on the desk that used to be hers.

I stare out of the window at the heavy sky, then down at a clogged artery of traffic on the Westway. The road is always jammed, a constant coagulation of traffic and bodies in and out of London every minute of the day. How depressing to have to commute every day in and out of this crowded city. I can't see the faces of the people in their cars, just dark shapes, arms, watches, brake lights pulsing in the dusk.

My mobile phone vibrates and I glance down at the text message on its screen.

'What time are you getting to A's?'

I don't want to go to A's party. I feel heavy and worn down and the early dark and the sight of the commuters fleeing the city has sucked something out of me. Is it that? Or is there something else wrong? I'm not sure. My mood is darkening and I know already where I want to take it. I said I'd be there, and I don't want to let him down. But I just don't want to go. I can't face it. But nor do I want to go home to the flat. That would be dangerous. I look back at my list. The words stare back at me from the page, accusing.

Don't even think about it, I tell myself.

I close my eyes and press my thumb and forefinger into my eyelids so I'm plunged into a red and black darkness through which I feel myself falling. The front part of my skull dissolves and a large chocolate brownie materialises unbidden from somewhere around my temporal lobes and floats, majestically, richly brown, into the centre of my vision. It's the kind they have in the supermarket just around the corner. I see the way it darkens at the bottom, the changing densities of it, the way it flakes at the top. I devour it, gobbling it up, big mouthfuls at a time. My mouth is salivating, my pulse racing.

I force my eyes open and pull out a document. Printed words swim on the page. Figures. It's a breakdown of where the money is coming from to fund the Games. I stare at the numbers angrily. Numbers have never been my forte. Why can I never remember how much of the Olympics' funding is coming from the National Lottery? What on earth is wrong with me? The numbers just won't go in. I move on to the next page, to a diagram of the proposed stadium, but through its sketched outlines all I can see are supermarket shelves crowded with the goodies I would buy, if I just gave myself in to this impulse. As I flip to the third page I can't help it, I bite into an imaginary croissant that has a soft almondy paste at its heart.

The office recedes. My colleagues are sucked away from me, vanishing into a parallel universe. My pulse quickens with excitement and anticipation.

All at once I'm in a room. In it is a low-slung sofa. Red, clean, functional, with no history. And a table within easy reaching distance. I'm alone. The temperature in the room is perfect. The room is not part of a house, it is unattached, just a room, anonymous, minimal. Nobody can enter the room. There is no phone, no television. Its lines are clean and simple. It is a peaceful place, serene, still. I sit down. Spread across the white surface of the table, like an illustration out of a children's story book, is a feast of foods: whole cakes covered in icing and stuffed full of cream, pyramids of cream cakes and cupcakes, sugar-dusted doughnuts with jam oozing out of small punctures in their roundness, mounds of iced biscuits, jugs of cream, pots of tea, chicken pies, pizzas under melted cheese.

In my fantasy I'm working my way through this feast, not shovelling it in in a frenzy, in a cold panic, but gently, steadily eating and eating and eating, with a plate and a fork, cutting myself huge wedges of cake and transferring them to my plate, drowning them in cream. I am treating myself, it is controlled, it is what I want and I will eat whatever I like, and as much as I like and for as long as I like. In the room there is none of the fear, the shame or the recrimination that always dog my binges.

This, I decide, is how I will carry out my binge tonight. I can leave this frustration behind, this feeling that I'm no good, that I'm in the wrong place, the feeling of being sucked out of myself when I look out of the window. I will smother it under layers and layers of creamy-spongy-chocolatey-feasting-gorging. I'll be all alone. The world will not be let in.

I've pressed so hard into my eyeballs that black dots shoot across my vision. There's a small noise and through a retreating darkness I see Fran standing opposite me, looking down at me quizzically.

'Are you all right, Jonesy?'

'Yes, I'm fine!' I straighten, seize my pencil, scratch a circle around one of the figures on the page. The feast vanishes.

I busy myself with the diagram of the stadium as she readies herself to leave. Don't do it, I warn myself. I'll be exhausted tomorrow if I do it. And I'll have to tell Penny; I'll have to tell Penny how pathetic . . .

'Night, Jonesy,' she says.

'Night, Fran,' I say.

'See you tomorrow.'

'No, I'm filming with Ben in Manchester tomorrow. Our lifer gets out of prison and we might be up there for a few days, depending what happens.'

Fran doesn't look too happy about the arrangement.

'But I'll be here on Monday. And you can reach me on my mobile at any time if you need anything.'

'Great.' She smiles, relaxing, letting go of the day. 'Have a nice evening.'

'You too, Fran.' I smile back.

As she walks away I press my fingers into my temples, head down.

Breathe, I tell myself. Ignore it. It might go away.

I look up to see the assistant doing the rounds of the office with a box of biscuits someone has brought back from a sunny holiday elsewhere. Now she's next to me, the box in the air between us. She has straight blonde hair, she's curvy, happy, efficient. As she talks she waves the box around in the air between us.

Without allowing myself to resist I take a biscuit and eat it quickly. It tastes so good, so sweet. I take another. She walks back to her desk. I watch her place the box of biscuits on top of the office fridge, open. I am ravenously, uncontainably hungry.

'Does anyone want anything?' I stand up. 'I'm going to get some chocolate from the shop.' They all shake their heads, already on the last stretch before home. I can smell their comfortable homes on them, their kitchens and boyfriends and husbands, their secure, contained evenings ahead of them.

I enter the lift and turn my back on my reflection. The first thing I'm going to put in my wire basket is the chocolate brownie that lives in the bakery section, three paces down in the right-hand aisle.

The lift doors open onto the ground floor. Harish is at the security turnstile between me and the sliding doors that lead out of the building, his security uniform tight over his large belly.

'Half day, Jonesy?'

I smile at him with an attempt to look rueful. 'I wish! Just going to the shop. Want anything?'

'No, thanks,' he looks at his watch stretched across his wide wrist. 'I'm out of here in ten minutes. Anyway, let me know if you want to come to my club night on Saturday, OK?'

'Thanks, Harish. I'll let you know.'

I'm out of the sliding doors, around the corner of the building and just moments away from the supermarket doors. I'll buy myself one of those long boxes of cream cakes. I don't always buy them on a binge, because they're expensive, but this late in the day they might be reduced. On this round I'll just buy what I can easily eat at my desk. Later, when I leave for home, I'll buy the rest of it.

I pick up chocolate bars and packets of custard creams, put them back, pick them up again. Perhaps some of those round ridged biscuits with caramel inside them, the ones that come in a see-through plastic packet. Or Orange Clubs. Mr Kipling's Bakewell Tarts are on offer. I put them in my basket. I stare at a coffee cake, a Madeira cake, a chocolate loaf cake, and put a big pot of double cream in my basket. I return the cream to the shelf – that's for later when I'm at home. I can pour the entire pot over a cake. I go to the pastry section and fill a bag with almond croissants and chocolate brownies. I work fast. I have to get back to my desk and I don't want to be seen in here, not with all this food.

It isn't the first time I've managed to begin a binge before I've even left the building. I'll buy a bag of food and place it slightly opened on the floor under my desk. Nobody notices if I lift out one chocolate bar after another, one biscuit at a time, head down, working, diligent. Soon they'll all be packing up to go home. There'll be the odd person still in the office putting together their camera kit for the following day, adding the last touches to the call sheet, phoning America.

As I head back towards the building I see, off to my right, Harish ambling down the broad concrete walkway to the road, the tops of his thighs rubbing together. I picture him walking like this all the way to the home he shares with his elderly Indian parents and a nephew. It's a squeeze in his house. He told me this over roast chicken in the canteen at lunchtime. I picture him oversized in a small bedroom, eating pizza and watching television late into the night, and dreaming about the new job he's applied for in marketing. We worked on his application over lunch. He'd be great in marketing. I hope he gets the job.

Later on when I finally leave for home I buy a loaf of bread and a packet of butter. Toast is good security food at the end of a binge if I run out of other binge food. I buy the pot of cream too, the biggest one. I deliberate over the cream because it's expensive. I hate spending money on my binges but I have to, so I try to economise. I decide on the chocolate loaf cake. I pick up a two-litre bottle of semi-skimmed milk. The milk looks clean and tasteless next to the binge food in my basket. The cream cakes are discounted now, so I buy a whole box – an apple puff, two éclairs and a cream slice look out through the box's plastic window. I also buy a giant chocolate bar, three packets of biscuits: custard creams, chocolate bourbons, and Maryland chocolate chips, which are only thirty-five pence today. I pick up a Bakewell tart. The pastries are on offer, in plastic bags with red stickers on them. I put a bag in the basket. I can't risk not having enough, but I don't like not being able to finish all the binge food – I don't like waste. I decide to leave the Bakewell tart. I stare at a tin of beans. I'll need some real food when this is all over but I just can't do it. I can't buy anything practical during my binge-food buying – those areas of my life must remain separate. I go to the checkout with my full basket: £8.75.

It's dark outside now. I exit the sliding doors, tearing open the cream cakes with my hand buried in the plastic bag. I walk fast and eat solidly all the way home, past the stadium, past the park, along the residential street, across the busy main road, not looking to left or right, not making eye contact with the kids on bikes, the demented old woman I once spoke to at the launderette, whose bag of laundry I'd ended up carrying for her back to her dingy basement flat that smelled of old clothes and neglect. She'd sat on her narrow bed, her tights sagging around her knees, and watched me with evident confusion and mounting suspicion as I laid out her clothes on her dresser as quickly as I could.

At Shepherd's Bush I board a bus that grunts its way southward as I stare out of the window, my back to the other passengers, reaching in and out, in and out of the plastic bag. I jump off on the Brompton Road and cut across the cemetery. I don't notice the headstones today, the grey, mossed crosses tilting this way and that on the uneven earth; I don't see the domed chapel. I march out of the south gates, and head down towards the Thames and the flat I rent from my uncle.

I unlock the front door, flick on the kettle, pull a plate and a fork and a bowl out of the cupboard, drop two slices of bread into the toaster, cut a huge slice of cake, drown it in cream then march to the living room and turn on the television. I switch off my mobile phone, lay the food out in front of me. It's just me and the food, and the noise of the television helps me to stop thinking about what I'm doing.

Two hours in, and as if for the first time I look up and see myself. I'm surrounded by the food debris. Empty packets and torn wrappers are littered across the table and the floor. The cakes have gone. There is no cream left, no cream cakes, no pastries; just the empty containers they came in. I am most of the way through the third packet of biscuits. And now it's beginning to really hurt. I think how insane this would look to someone watching. I'm disgusting, a freak. I eat more and more because now I just want to get to the end and get all this food out of me. I flick between channels, desperate to find something that will keep my attention focused outward. I drink more cups of tea because it helps to make the food liquid in my stomach, and easier to vomit out at the end. But I don't think about what I have to do at the end of this, I just keep eating and trying to keep thoughts out of my head.

It is late. Three or four hours have passed and I have eaten without a pause. I have taken in all the food I can cram into my stomach and I'm so bloated and distended that it hurts – that's usually a good thing because the discomfort or the nausea or both means I'll get the nasty end job over and done with sooner. The skin between my ribs and my stomach is stretched taut.

I go to the bathroom and stare at myself in the mirror. To delay what I have to do I start examining my face, picking at it, pulling faces. I try on makeup – I don't wear lipstick but I put some on and grin at myself in the mirror. I turn sideways to look at myself that way. If I am ever pregnant, that's what I'll look like, slim arms, strong wiry legs, but a huge bulge of a stomach. I put my hand on my lower back and waddle around back and forth, still in front of the mirror. Maybe that's how you walk when you're eight months pregnant.

Reluctantly, I get down to business. There's nothing else I can think of doing that will put it off any longer. And I have to do it because all that food is waiting to come out. I wash my hands, bend over the toilet and stick my fingers down my throat until I gag. The first wave of saliva washes down the inside of my cheeks. The first vomit is painful, but the second is a relief. I vomit until I can't any more and what I'm tasting isn't concentrated chocolate but bile.

I wash my face, rinse out my mouth with water several times. I can't brush my teeth yet because I have to wait until my saliva has neutralised the abrasive stomach acid that is now in my mouth so that it doesn't damage the enamel on my teeth.

It's over. My hands are shaking and my throat is sore. I lean my forehead on the cool edge of the sink and stay there. I feel exhausted and numb. I consider lying down on the cool bathroom floor and sleeping there. I feel too tired to walk to my bedroom. I feel too tired to wash my face and prepare for bed, to ready my bag and my camera kit for the pre-dawn start the following day, charging batteries and cleaning lenses, picking up as though this was just the tail-end of an ordinary day, of anyone else's ordinary day.

That kind of normality feels light years away from me: the normality of an evening after work in the city – home on the tube, cook, clear up the kitchen, continue with the book I'm reading, watch a programme, pull the weeds out of the pots in the courtyard, have a glass of wine, chat with one of my friends or my mum or my dad or my siblings, get ready for bed.

The things normal people do. The idea that I could do those things without the alter ego in me fighting for a different kind of reality altogether, fighting to ambush, is too far away from where I am. So I stay there, with my forehead on the cool sink.

I feel so much worse than I did before I decided to binge. The mania has drained away, leaving me settled at rock bottom. But this is the part I always used to forget, before I got better – that the end is so much worse. That I may have escaped from my frustration and my fears at four o'clock on a Tuesday afternoon, that I may have activated my get-out-of-jail-free card and slipped away to a place with no requirements for restraint or balance or sanity, but I've ended up with a body that is bruised and a mood that is sinking deeper and deeper into darkness. And now that it's all over I am even further away from being able to resolve any of the problems that got me here in the first place. I don't even know what they are. When they next arise my reaction will be the same, to lose myself through food.

Because the crazy thing is, it works. Bingeing works. It takes me out of claustrophobia, out of boredom, away from stress and anxiety and anger. It takes me away from my lack of compass. It leaves me empty and in pain, but it does get me away, for a moment, from all those other intolerable monsters. And when they come back I resort to the same trusted mechanism of escape because, after fourteen years of doing it like this, I know no other way of staying afloat.

Two

The following day in Manchester.
March 2006

Chris Banks was inside for murder. The day we met him it was his first day of freedom in twenty-eight years. It was 9 a.m. and Ben, the director, and I had been driving since before dawn to make sure we got to the prison near Manchester in plenty of time. We'd seen the colour of the sky change over the hunched frame of the prison as we waited, Ben bent over his camera on its tripod while I watched for any signs of movement on the other side of the prison gates, stamping my feet to keep warm. We'd been told he might come out at nine, but that it sometimes took longer to process the inmates, sometimes an extra hour or two. No telling, the prison officer on the phone had told me.

When he did emerge it was anticlimactic. There was a big clanking gate which I'd hoped would open portentously, the way they do in films, but just as a light rain began to fall our lifer emerged out of a small side gate with a plastic bin liner of his

17

belongings over his shoulder. His mother wailed, mostly for our benefit, I think, and they hugged. Then the four of us got into the car to drive back to their house.

Back at the house the three-legged dog had peed on the carpet, not for the first time. Chris's mother settled her weight back into its groove on the sofa and Chris sat beside her to watch a film, smoking roll-ups and complaining about the size of the screen, answering in monosyllables the questions Ben asked about coming home. Just as the film started Chris ran down the road to the chip shop to get some chips for their tea, which they ate, without speaking, as the action movie unrolled. We decided to call it a day, and promised to be back early the next morning to spend Chris's first full day of freedom with him.

Chris had told us he wanted to try to track down his sons, who had disowned him and moved to another part of Manchester when they were old enough to understand that their Dad was inside for murder. But the next morning he decided to go to the Asda superstore instead. While he was in prison he had been injured in an accident in the carpentry workshop and had received a small compensation. It was all the money he had, apart from the dole he would be collecting once he had signed on. His brother, also an ex-convict – armed robbery in his case – drove us to Asda, where they found the largest TV screen in the store and carted it home. As he assembled it we asked him questions about his plans, and how it felt to be out. It seemed to us both from what he told us, and he concurred, that there wasn't much difference between being inside and being outside, except the food was better outside.

Ben and I spent the next three days in Chris's front room with the odds and ends of his extended family and the three-legged dog, trying to coax something watchable out of his experience of coming home. We hung around, drinking tea on the sofa, watching daytime TV, boiling the kettle, avoiding dogshit in the backyard, following him down to the Pakistani corner shop to buy tobacco, waiting for something, anything, to happen, that would give us a clue as to how Chris's story might unfold. I watched the Pakistani man, who looked to be in his fifties, standing behind the counter at the corner shop; I wondered where he came from in Pakistan. I wanted to ask him how he ended up here, of all places. I wanted to tell him that I lived in Islamabad as a teenager, in the F72 quarter near Jinnah market. I'd tell him some of the details of our lives there. I'd tell him about my school, and I'd tell him I stole my parents' car in the middle of the night and drove to Faisal Mosque, crouched, huge, lit up, ready for blast-off with its minarets pointing up into space. I'd tell him how beautiful the mosque looked at night, because he would like that. But I never managed to talk to him; there wasn't the right time. Chris would buy his tobacco and we'd return to the house.

When we tired of waiting for things to happen Ben and I excused ourselves and drove around the grim, lifeless streets of the neighbourhood with the windows down, discussing how we could breathe life into the film, broaden it out to be a profile of a criminal underworld in a deprived suburb of Manchester. Perhaps we were being too impatient. Something was bound to happen sooner or later. Perhaps the editor in London would give us some leeway, a little more time to find our way to what the story was really about. We'd return to the house, inspired again. But there he'd be with his prison pallor, slouched on the sofa in the grey air of the front room, the kettle on, another roll-up between his missing front teeth, eyes on the telly, content.

At the end of each day we drove to a lonely house Ben's aunt owned out in the Peak District, not far from Manchester; it was filled with her books and handwritten journals detailing her walks across the moorlands and craggy hills of the Dark Peak. Retreating to our separate rooms, we'd try to reconnect with our other lives. I'd hear Ben's muffled voice through the walls as he spoke to his wife and kids.

On the Friday we bade goodbye to the Banks family, promising to return soon to continue filming.

It's dark by the time we arrive home. Ben drops me at my flat and speeds off into the night. I open the front door to the empty flat, to the stillness of the blue sofa, and the houseplants unmoving under the skylight. Everything holding its breath. I have looked forward to coming home, to being on my own again, to escaping from the claustrophobic inertia of our days in the North, but all the gathered expectation turns to something else as I walk in; I feel it happening but I try to ignore it.

I throw my things down on the bed, walk once around the rooms, treading quietly in the stillness, stopping beneath the gilt-framed paintings of British ancestors whose names I don't know and a black and white photograph of my Palestinian grandmother, my mother's mother. My grandmother met and married my grandfather, a British army officer, in Palestine at the start of the Second World War. When they decided to marry, my grandmother sent this photograph of herself, with her brother Maurice, to her soon-to-be mother-in-law in England. She wanted her to see that Palestinians are sophisticated, educated people too.

I know the picture well. She is standing on a terrace of her house with her back to the Bay of Haifa, smiling at the camera, red-lipsticked, her hat tilted sideways. The city, far below her, a jumble of indistinct white houses and other buildings, stretches out towards the sea. Maurice, holding a cigarette, is squinting into the bright day, wearing a smart white suit; a beautiful man, like his sister and like my mother, who is the eldest of my grandmother's five children. My grandmother looks young in the photo, perhaps the age I am now. On the back, in a careful cursive she must have learned in her French convent school in Haifa, she wrote, simply: 'This is my brother Maurice.'

For a suspended moment I stand and look at these old familiar faces that used to peer down at us in my grandmother's flat, where I spent so much time when I first came to England from Africa at sixteen. When my grandmother died she passed on the family paintings and photographs to my uncle, her eldest son, and here they are in his flat.

I breathe in the familiar smell of the place, open up the kitchen window into the little courtyard. I stand looking out at the plants – a rubber plant, a yucca growing too big for its pot, plants crowding upwards towards their little patch of London sky.

I could fill this unfilled space; I could take a bath, listen to music, catch up with my friends, call my parents. I could have a glass of wine. This could be another free day, another clear day.

But it's too quiet and I'm too tired to resist. I'm so tired, I even lack the imagination to think of an alternative to my evening. So I pull a fistful of plastic bags out of the cupboard under the sink and walk out into the London night. I cut across the World's End Estate and turn left to the nearest supermarket, a Co-op, my mouth already watering in anticipation; my mind, not empty or struggling against an encroaching loneliness, but instead filled with the thrill of what I will eat on my binge, anything I like, as much as I like, with no boundaries.

Later that night, sick with myself, I hold the remains of the junk food under the running tap before pushing it to the bottom of the bin. I do that so that I can't on a sudden impulse pick it out of the rubbish later or the next day to start another binge.

The last thing I do before I sleep is fill in my entries in the blue diary. I have been keeping these diaries, slim blue diaries that I carry everywhere with me, ever since I started seeing Penny at an eating-disorders unit in South London. In them I record everything I eat, when I ate it, and what I was feeling or thinking at the time. Penny gives me a new one each week to fill in. I flick back through the pages of this week's: Monday: bad; Tuesday, Wednesday and Thursday: good. Today, Friday: bad. It's a shame, because I was doing so well, I was making progress. I had an invincible first month, with days and days at a time free from bingeing, high on the sudden realisation that this problem I had was a real thing, and a thing that could be fixed, here, now, with Penny's help. I knew then, for the first time, that everything was going to change. But I'm in the third month now, and I've fallen down. Penny warned it might happen, that it might get bad again before it gets better.

It's Friday and I see Penny on Monday. I long to be there in the quiet of the small square space of her room, making some sense of the week. Right now it seems senseless, chaotic. I feel I have lost all control, my days spinning away from me into this black hole. I feel my self-control, my force of will, my clarity, slipping away.

But I'll be OK for the next few days, I must be OK. I promise myself I will be OK, I will break out of this repeating cycle.

I finish recording my binge. I turn off the bedside light, bid goodnight to my grandmother, there in the photo, and I pray she hasn't, from wherever she is, witnessed what I have done.

This is my brother Maurice

Teta in Palestine, 1939.

Three

Three weeks later at my parents' home in Sussex.
April 2006

I'm busying about my bedroom, immersed in a satisfying monotony of morning tasks: I've already opened wide the thick curtains onto the sunny day, I've wiped away a cobweb from the window frame, I've peered out into the garden at the spring sunshine playing on the daffodils and stood quietly for a few moments by the window in the welcome silence of the countryside. My weekend bag is open and empty on the floor, the clothes already hung up and folded away in the cupboard in the corner that my father and I painted when my parents first moved into this house six years ago on their return from Africa.

I close the cupboard doors and touch the simple matt white with my fingertips. A fragment of a line from a Spanish song drifts to me from memory. As my father and I painted the cupboard and then the white walls of the room that was to be my bedroom in this new home in England, we memorised the words of a Spanish song and repeated them back to each other, line by line, verse by verse until we knew it all by heart. It was Dad's idea, not mine. It took us most of the morning to get right, as it was not a simple song but an old-fashioned folksong full of archaic language and melancholic musings on fate and tragedy. As well as an entertaining way of passing the hours as the room grew gradually whiter and our verses more robust, it was an exercise in my father's lifelong quest to improve his Spanish, and by roping me in he could achieve the added covert advantage of improving my Spanish too.

I turn from the cupboard to the crumpled bed. The song was called 'María La Portuguesa' – that much I remember. As I'm plumping up the pillows, the first line comes back to me:

'*En las noches de luna y clavel . . .*'

The line bothers me because I don't know what '*clavel*' means, and I'm fairly certain it's a word I would never use in ordinary conversation, but it sticks there, disturbing the fluid poetry of the first verse. I smooth out the duvet and try to recall the story. María fell in love with an unsuitable man, their love was 'consummated' down by the river on a night of 'passion and sighs', and then she died. She may have been killed. Or perhaps *he* died, not her. I can't remember. More fragments of verse are coming back to me now. I pick the bedspread off the floor and shake it once so that it billows over the bed. As it settles with a sigh of air, Anna appears in the doorway and asks me if I've seen the thing in the kitchen.

Anna is covering her mouth with her slender hand. Her hands are more evenly shaded than mine, her fingernails short and clean and uniformly shaped. I have our father's practical hands, thin fingers and wide knuckles. I look blankly at my sister.

Anna is only thirteen months older than I am and I don't usually need to ask her to know what she is thinking; in fact, much of the time I don't even need to look at her to know what she is thinking. The fabric of our days was the same until we went to boarding school and our paths diverged. Same dogs, same way of doing backflips, same number of steps we could take on our hands in a handstand, same mud animal figures we'd try to sell at the end of our driveway to poor Kenyan kids on their way back from school, same made-up songs from the back of the Kenyan cereal packet, the one with a picture of a sun on it:

> Dates, raisins, honey nuts,
> rolled oats, barley, ee, tee, cee.

Even now we'll be walking along together and she'll suddenly stop, hold out her hand to stop me too, to pin down a smell that comes to us from somewhere, that pulls us back to childhood. 'What is it?' she'll ask. We'll be in London, the traffic spinning around us.

'Sudan?' I'll suggest. 'Is it the bread we used to eat there, with the weevils in it?' She shakes her head.

We've both stopped, breathing deeply.

'Ugali?' I ask. Ugali was the maize porridge our ayah ate every day. Anna shakes her head, then she smiles.

'Pro Nutro,' she says. She has a better smell-memory than me.

We breathe it in deeply, this smell that's like the smell of the baby cereal we ate in Lesotho before we moved to Kenya. It's the smell of our Lesotho kitchen, that's what it is.

But now I look blankly at my sister. I'm relieved to see that underneath her hand she is suppressing a nervous smile, so it's serious, but a compromised sort of serious, more serious for me, probably, than for her.

And then I remember: Dad. This must have something to do with what Dad has in store for us this morning: the family summit. Today is the day Dad wants us to talk about my illness. He wants to talk about it because by now I've been seeing Penny for nearly three months. And my father, and probably the rest of the family, feel that we should be drawing some useful conclusions about what is going on – where all this disorder in my life came from and what we can do about it and what they can do to help me.

I know that I woke early this morning as a faint light crept around the edge of the curtains, and in the still air of my bedroom my thoughts gathered anxiously, tadpole-like, around the prospect of having to talk to my family about my illness. I hoped Dad might have forgotten or gone for a long bike ride, or perhaps arranged a last-minute game of squash. By the time I awoke the second time I had put the family gathering out of my head and replaced thoughts of it with the repeating fragments of verses of 'María La Portuguesa'.

Anna drops her hand from her mouth. 'So have you seen it?' she asks.

'No.' I chew my bottom lip. 'What is it?'

Anna turns and walks down the hallway towards the kitchen, so I follow her. She stops when she enters the kitchen, and stands with her hands on her hips. The clock ticks on the wall, steam rises from the still-hot kettle, birds flutter noiselessly outside. For a moment we stand side by side, in silence, staring. The flipchart stands in a pool of light slanting in from the windows, its empty white pages facing out over the long wooden table. In its sill lie two coloured pens, blue and red, and a ruler. Anna and I look at one another, then look back at the flipchart, unmoving, innocent, on its three-legged easel.

For nearly a decade I kept my illness secret from my family. But even after I finally told them the truth I still found it excruciating to try to talk about it. By the time my father slipped out of the house that sunny spring morning, took his bicycle out of the garden shed and, the air full of the promise of a new season, cycled smartly to the village stationer's to buy the flipchart, I had managed to avoid the subject for a few years.

Still, in spite of the unspoken rule that says we don't talk about it, every now and then one of them, unable to hold back, will bring it up. At once I feel I'm trapped in a rockpool with nowhere to hide. I feel myself closing up rapidly like one of those sticky sea anemones that can draw its red tentacles into its body so all you can see of it is a smooth, ordered roundness. I have tried to overcome my panic and I have tried to discuss it like an adult, thoughtfully, calmly, but I can't. I can't because I don't think I can answer the question I know they want to ask: Why? Why did this happen? And because I find it very hard to admit to weakness, to being so flawed. To admit, in real time, to not coping with life, this simple life full of abundance and privilege and the possibility of health. The possibility of health right there, within my reach, waiting for me to take it up.

So when they do ask, I know my answers rarely satisfy. Usually I try to reassure my mother or father or sister or brother that while there are hiccups, progress is being made. That I'm heading in the right direction. They look so immediately relieved and happy when I say this that I can't really stand to say anything else. And I'm adept at changing the subject too, most of the time.

I can sense it coming from all of them from a million miles off, but particularly from my father. It happens when we're alone, on one of my visits home from London, and it happened just this way yesterday.

For most of the morning it had rained. As soon as it began to clear Dad and I decided to go for a country walk. We marched down the lane with Wusha the dog on our way to a footpath, as we have done so many times. Dad gave me his arm, I tucked mine into his and he squeezed it against his side, holding my hand tightly.

We fall into step, me keeping pace with my father's strong, purposeful strides. He's looking slightly down at the ground towards his khaki-green wellies, which warns me that he is thinking about how to broach the subject. I am also looking down at our muddy boots squelching along over tarmac, fallen leaves and horse manure, and hoping for a last-minute reprieve.

I glance around us. The lane is empty. The trees are holding leafy branches up against a sky struggling to retrieve its blue through the clouds. The dog runs up and down the lane, disappears amongst the farm buildings, then re-emerges around the side of the handsome brick barn. Dad is still squeezing my hand; we're heading for the stile which will take us away from the lane and into open fields. I glance sideways at his face to check if I'm right about what is coming. His grey eyes are serious; he looks troubled, lost in thought. Two more paces and then it comes.

'So how are you?' Dad asks, pulling me even more tightly against his side, as though to transfer some of his considerable strength over to me.

'Fine, thanks,' I answer. We take a few more steps, squelching over more leaves and mud. He says nothing.

I don't know if he heard me. He lost some of his hearing in the army years ago, before I was born. Before he and my mother moved to Africa with the International Red Cross during Biafra, the Nigerian civil war, he was an officer in the artillery regiment. The loud explosions damaged his hearing.

'I'm OK,' I then say a little more honestly, a little more firmly, into his silence. Some small yellow fruit are scattered across the road. I crush one under foot. It spills its yellow insides across the road.

And then I break. 'Not bad,' I admit. It comes out weakly.

Then Dad turns his face to me and smiles encouragingly.

'And how's the Bully?'

He called it 'the Bully'. He once asked me, when I told him how hard it was to stop the behaviour once I'd felt the urge to do it, whether I would be able to let him know in a coded way if I was feeling vulnerable by saying to him, 'The Bully is back.' He would understand what I meant, even if others didn't, and then we could act together to save the day. I told him I didn't think that would work. I don't think he understood why not – it was a simple, clear system – and I could not find the words to explain why it wouldn't. He said that if I didn't want to say it aloud then we could come up with an alternative way of alerting him to trouble ahead, perhaps a simple hand signal. He had held up his strong brown hand, darkened by the sun as it rested on the open car window frame, and waved it in the air to demonstrate.

I never did employ the hand signal to warn my father that I was being overtaken by a desire to binge. It just doesn't work that way for me, even though perhaps it should.

How is the Bully? I think back to the previous week. It was pretty bad. Three evenings gone.

'Not bad,' I say. 'You know, up and down a bit.'

'Has it been happening recently?'

'Yes. A few times. I had a bad patch a couple of weeks ago. But I'm over it now. I feel OK really.'

I know that I'm lying, but I can't talk about it in the present tense. It has to be in a contained past, a compound past tense, for actions completed in the past, not leaking imperfectly into the present. We squelch past two horses hanging their heads over a gate into the lane. They watch us silently as we walk by.

I blink back tears. I can't help it. I can't help feeling pitifully, miserably sorry for myself. Will I ever be free of this? In this moment I cannot remember ever being free and I cannot even imagine what it would feel like. It will not happen to me.

After the stile I'll be able to breathe. Left. Right. Left. Right. I find myself repeating the marching ditty Dad once taught me,

> I had a good friend and I Left, Left, Left.
> It jolly well served me Right, Right, Right.

But we aren't marching fast enough as we approach the stile to keep it going.

Breathe in, I tell myself. Keep breathing. I must put a positive spin on this. Think of Penny. Think of that patch of blue carpet between my chair and her feet.

We're at the stile. Dad lets go of me and in that moment of

reprieve as we are about to climb over into the open space of the fields beyond I find an even breath, draw all my shreds of courage together at the back of my throat, and say:

'I know I'm getting better, Dad. Thanks to Penny. Penny has been really great.'

He squeezes my arm with his strong hand. 'Well done, Daughter. I'm very proud of you, you know.'

I nod to let him know that I know.

We both climb over the stile. At this point the view opens up to the left, to the Sussex Downs stretching away towards the sea. Wusha runs off, searching for smells along a field of stubbly stalks. He stops at a point where I once saw a badger, a beautiful English badger, stumble out of the undergrowth and disappear into the farmer's field. It was evening and I stood still as the light faded, hoping he would come back.

We start climbing towards a second stile at the crest of the hill.

'It's just that it's a bit of a journey.' I have to raise my voice so Dad can hear me above the rush of the wind. And the volume of my voice makes me sound less tentative. 'Penny says there are bound to be ups and downs. I think that's just part of the process of getting better. But there's no question that I'm better than I was before. Much better.' This is true, and it bolsters me. Since I started seeing Penny everything is changing. This is just a stumble. It is still early days. I mustn't forget the extraordinary clumps of days, of wellness, I've had since I started seeing Penny. They began almost immediately.

'Excellent news,' Dad says. 'Penny has altogether been excellent news, hasn't she?'

'Yes!' I shout.

I'm happy to be out of the lane. The lane feels like England to me, but up here with the wider views and the wind and the dome of the sky above it starts to feel wilder, freer. Dad and I are no longer bent forwards, contained, watching the ground in front of us. We've opened up, we're looser and striding and the wind is making my clothes flap against me. I pull off my hat and my long hair blows around my head.

'This does me the world of good, getting out into the fresh air on a day like today,' Dad shouts over the wind.

'Me too!' I call back. I can feel my mood lifting out here on the hillside.

'Can't be cooped up in the house all day,' he says. 'Need to get the blood pumping.'

I point at a field of tender stems coming up through the soil. This field is always changing with the seasons and I can't keep up with it.

'What are they growing here?'

'It's corn,' he says. '"Maize" as we called it in Africa.'

We climb up past the fields of maize towards a second stile up at the crest. Dad points to the southeast, and I know what he's about to say:

'See that ring of trees over there on that hill?'

I nod.

'That's Chanctonbury Ring.'

Dad's face has reddened slightly with the wind. Even after all these years I'm still not used to seeing him here in a cold climate, wrapped up in scarf, hat and gloves in the winter. All his clothes in Africa were lightweight in inconspicuous beige or khaki. I'm used to seeing him in the same style of trousers he bought from the same shop on Muindi Mbingu Street in

Nairobi for thirty years. Or in the white T-shirt and shorts and Hi-Tec trainers he wears to play squash. He was always in control of the game, his muscular brown arms and legs invincible. He always won his games. He still does, even now at sixty-five. His skin is still dark.

'All those years in the African sun,' he says, whenever I point this out.

We reach the second stile.

'So is Penny's therapy providing you with any answers?' he asks.

'Yes, I think so. Well, definitely, yes. But it's not that easy to explain, Dad. Sorry. It's complicated.'

Then as we leave the maize fields and climb down through the woods where there are bluebells in the spring, Dad, unusually, does not let it go. He asks me if when we get home we can all sit down to talk about it; and emboldened by the wind, the open sky and the stems of maize easing through soil, and the clumps of wellness that have stretched and receded, then reappeared again these past months, I say yes.

Now I'm back in my bedroom, sitting on my almost made bed. And all I can think about is the flipchart in the kitchen. I can hear my parents moving about upstairs and it seems to me there is a different sound to their movements this morning. There's anticipation in the creaking ceiling joists. My throat is tight. I rub my toe over a patch of carpet thinned by moths.

The murmur of Radio 4's *Today* programme drifts down the stairs. My parents' curtains will be open, the bed made and the binoculars on the bedside table. I can hear their voices, quietly. Perhaps my mother is asking Father to recall some detail brought up by the news programme they are listening to – the name of a Somali warlord he knew, for example, from our days in Ethiopia when Somalia was in a constant and chaotic state of war, which grew the refugee camps on the Ethiopia–Somalia border; or what happened to the glamorous Swedish count who fought as a mercenary for the Biafrans in Nigeria, where my parents moved to just weeks after they were married. Count Von Rosen, Dad told us, considered a hero by the Biafrans, flew MFI9s, small civilian acrobatic planes better suited to loop-the-loops than to warfare, against the Nigerian forces. He modified the undersides of the planes' wings to carry rockets and attacked from the air, while Dad, on the ground, coordinated medical relief teams for the International Red Cross, helping both sides in the conflict. Dad told us that Von Rosen's rockets weren't always terribly effective, not against the MiGs of the Nigerian Air Force, anyway. He laughed when he told us the story of Von Rosen's attack on Enugu airport: the only casualty was the poor customs officer, who fell into a ditch while running away and broke his leg. My parents both loved Nigeria, especially Enugu, a city that reverted to bush during the war.

The Count turned up again in Ethiopia a while later, in 1974, the year I was born in Addis Ababa; he was working with my father who was by then distributing food aid for the Relief Commission. This time Von Rosen had converted his civilian planes to carry sacks of grain instead of rockets, and he was able to fly up to the flat-topped Ethiopian hills that were difficult to access by road, and drop bags of grain to famine-affected areas. The method they helped to pioneer, double-bagging, was later used to drop far greater quantities of food from bigger, Hercules aircraft – the tight inner bag holding the grain would split on impact, leaving the loose outer one intact. In the end, Dad told us, Von Rosen was killed on the flat roof of a hotel in Dire Dawa, out in that barren part of Ethiopia near Somalia, when Somali *shifta* attacked.

Or perhaps up there in their bedroom Mum is wondering about the circumstances of General Zia of Pakistan's assassination, which closed our school in Islamabad for a week. My sister and I didn't care about Zia. We had just arrived in Pakistan, a strange, hard country after Kenya, and when we heard the news we jumped up and down on the beds of the hotel we were living in while my parents looked for a house to rent. At least it meant we didn't have to go back to the school, where we had no friends.

Or perhaps they're commenting on the beautiful day; or my mother is standing by the windows, the binoculars trained on a great spotted woodpecker.

An hour later, we three women – my mother, my sister and I – are sitting at the kitchen table, waiting for my father, who is looking for his pointer in his study. The study walls are papered with charts and navigational maps of Africa.

'Don't you think this is a very good way of doing things?' Mum asks, nodding her head encouragingly at her girls.

'Maybe,' I say dubiously.

Anna sits back in her chair and folds her hands over her stomach. She is going to reserve judgement. Anna is not so easily drawn into agreement as I am.

'He is good, your father,' Mum says.

Dad enters the kitchen and takes his place by the flipchart. He extends the pointer to half-length.

'OK, Daughter,' he begins. 'We want to do this because we all want to understand more about your bulimia.'

This is fair. I have never actively wanted to keep news of my progress, or lack of it, from them; it's just that it has been so hard – impossible, really – to talk about. I can't take my eyes off the line of coloured pens in the sill of the flipchart and I'm back in Uganda, in my father's office in downtown Kampala. He had a flipchart covered with writing in one corner of his large office, and on the maps and charts hanging from the walls, arrows and figures showed the movement of refugees and the paths of ships and trucks and planes carrying food and medical supplies. By then he was directing operations for a vast swathe of East Africa, the countries spanning the Great Lakes of the Eastern Rift Valley, spreading outward from Lake Victoria, and getting food and supplies to hundreds of thousands of hungry people: Hutus in Eastern Zaire, Uganda and Tanzania, fleeing the crisis in Rwanda; and Ugandans in the north of the country in camps set up to provide refuge from the Lord's Resistance Army operating on the Sudan border. There he was in Kampala, in his ironed shirt, his desk uncluttered, handsome and in control in the clear, calm air of the office.

'If you can tell us more about it,' Dad goes on, 'we'll understand it better and we might be able to think of ways we can help.'

And with that he reveals the first page of the flipchart and I realise that he has already written headings at the tops of the pages. He has broken it down into pre-prepared categories.

'So I've broken it down into what I see as the major factors in the past, in your childhood in other words . . .' Dad points at the heading on the first page. 'ENVIRONMENTAL FACTORS:

BEFORE' is written in his spare capital letters. 'And' – he lifts
the top sheet so we can see the second page – 'the environmental
factors now.'

'ENVIRONMENTAL FACTORS: NOW', also in capital
letters, spans the top of the second page.

'Dad,' I interrupt. I can't help myself. 'I don't know if break-
ing it down into categories like this is, well, helpful.' Dad looks
disappointed. 'I mean, it's more complicated than that. I don't
know if I can easily put it into these different categories.'

Dad lowers the pointer to his side.

'Can I try to explain it in my way?'

He looks surprised, and pleased.

'Yes, of course you can, of course you can.' He hands me a
coloured pen quickly, in case I change my mind, and I stand up to
take his place at the flipchart. He sits in the chair I've just vacated.
There is silence as the three of them remain still, waiting.

The only thing I can think of doing is to recreate a picture
Professor Lacey, the consultant at the eating-disorders unit,
scribbled down for me on a piece of paper when I met him at
the hospital not long ago, just before my very first meeting with
Penny. From a desk piled with papers he had pulled out an
envelope and on the back of it had sketched a cake with
three layers.

Anna drove me to the hospital that day. I was thirty, and it was
the first time in ten years, ever since a short series of meandering
and ineffective monologues with a psychoanalyst at Oxford,
that I had sought professional help. It was the first time ever,
in fourteen years of struggling with the illness, that I had seen
a professional who was specifically trained in eating disorders.

Professor Lacey sat across from me at a large, dark desk. The type of desk that might be found in a barrister's office and have a green trim around its edge. It wasn't his office, it just happened to be free. I had filled in some questionnaires and the Professor flipped through them peremptorily, stopping at the odd question and probing me for more detail. His manner was not warm. It was challenging, almost impatient. He gave me the feeling that he was used to slippery customers and would tolerate no game-playing, no time-wasting. I answered his questions as honestly as I could, but he had seemed dissatisfied. I began to feel that I might be deluded. Perhaps being delusional was part of the condition. I knew I was a practised liar when it came to explaining my whereabouts, the hours and days that got swallowed up by my bingeing, the reasons for my disappearances and non-appearances, the general pretence that I was a normal person; but as I sat facing Professor Lacey, the old familiar feeling that I misunderstood the world in some fundamental way came back to me. He could probably see this as clearly as the aspidistra on the windowsill, its solitary purple flower straining towards the old windowpane. His manner did not alarm me. On the contrary, a small knot of hope grew under my ribs, where I imagine my sternum might be, that he might be able to provide me with some answers.

Professor Lacey tossed aside the questionnaire and asked me how I ended up coming to see him. I explained the sequence of events.

Just a week before I went to see the Professor, I had had what I can only describe as a breakdown, at a rainy bus stop in King's Cross. I'd been at a party and had missed the last tube home so was standing in the dark in the early hours amongst a crowd of people waiting for the night buses. After nearly an hour the number 10 appeared and approached the stop, pausing briefly at the pavement, but as I waited for the doors to open, Travelcard in hand, tightening my coat around me against the cold and the wet, the bus pulled away again into the night.

And then something finally gave, some bit of worn-thin fabric inside that is the difference between carrying on and not carrying on, and I found myself standing on the pavement screaming. I was not conscious of the people around me and what they might think of my hysteria as the Friday-night traffic slipped past. I caught up with the bus, pounded my fists against the doors as a sea of watery eyes peered at me through the rain-spattered glass, but the bus continued on its way.

Then, hearing shouting, my own shouting, I ran into the traffic to stop a taxi. All the other taxis I'd seen that night had been taken before I could reach them. The cab stopped, I slid into the back, collapsed into the corner, still crying, barely able to breathe, abandoned to a strange delirium. A concerned face looked back at me through the partition window. I spoke my address, then slipped back into my corner and my crying. It was then, as we pulled out into the traffic, all muffled sounds, red lights and rain streaming down the windows, that I heard a little disembodied voice coming from my bag. I took out my mobile phone and realised that in the confusion my sister's number must have dialled. Her name was on the screen and her voice was calling out. I hung up, horrified that she would have heard my wailing and shouting. The phone rang straight away. It was Anna. I had to answer it. I told her I had missed the bus, I told her I was safe. I told her I was in a taxi home and I promised to call her in the morning.

The next morning I called my parents and told them what was going on. They had known about my illness for some years by then – I had finally plucked up the courage to tell them after I left university and returned to our home in Uganda. I told my father and mother, my brother and sister, all at the same time, and all I wanted to think about that day was the way the light spilled onto my desk from the tree outside behind them, and the line of ants marching along the floor by the wall towards the window, and the thin patch in the white shorts I was wearing that I thought I might be able to poke through if I pushed hard enough. And then I settled on the final thought, the one I didn't want to think: that they would never see me in the same light again, as the words spilled, one by one, out of my mouth and into the room where I couldn't get them back. They would never again see me as the strong girl on the top diving-board, upside down a hand-stand, my fingers curled tightly over the end of the board, fearless. I'd felt that idea of myself softly collapse, in a puff of green mould dust. Gone.

After I'd told them, I had never again found the courage to be honest about the ongoing struggles I'd continued to have over the years that followed, until the night I missed the bus.

On the end of the line my father suggested he get straight into the car and drive to London to pick me up. He said I just had to say the word and he'd be there, day or night. I told them I'd been having a hard time with my eating, that it felt out of control again, I was depressed and I needed help. I had never asked them for help with my disorder before. Then, as Dad drove his Ugandan car up the motorway towards London to come and collect me, I called Anna and admitted to her that I did not think I could cope.

I told her about the events of the previous night, about how bad things had been. And in the long pause at the end of the conversation I admitted that I did not think I could survive with it in my life. I had never used language like that, and I knew how she would look: brown eyes steady, mouth closed, gently set; still, serious face, knowing that now the real thing was being said.

'This has gone on for too long,' she said.

It was my father who found the eating-disorders unit on the Internet, that very evening, and phoned them to request information. He passed it on to me and I contacted them. And that is how I found myself sitting opposite the prickling figure of Professor Lacey.

The Professor shook his head. 'The phone didn't dial itself. You called your sister.'

'No, it rang in my bag.' He must have misheard me. 'I didn't dial the number.'

He continued to shake his head. 'I think that's very unlikely. You called your sister. It was not an accident.'

I didn't call my sister. But I didn't argue; I felt that protesting would encourage his view of me, which I was beginning to perceive was of someone contrary and obstructive. Perhaps, I thought, eating-disordered patients are generally contrary and obstructive. And then, perhaps in some cosmic sense I did call out to my sister. Perhaps I had deliberately not locked the keypad when I put the phone in my bag, and my need for her help and the support of my family had translated itself into a movement of my body, which knocked my bag as I banged on the windows of the bus, which caused her number to be dialled.

Who knows? I don't usually go in for that kind of explanation, but I'm not ruling it out.

While Anna sat patiently in the coffee-smelling waiting room, Professor Lacey and I moved on from the question of whether or not I had deliberately called my sister to discuss antidepressants. He felt that antidepressants might help to get me back on my feet, but it was, he said, my decision. I had tried antidepressants before and I didn't think they had had any discernible impact on my eating disorder, and I wondered whether it wouldn't be better to begin the therapy with no masking factors. Did Professor Lacey think the antidepressants would help in my case? I wanted to know.

That was when he leaned across his desk, pulled out the envelope and drew the cake. It was a hastily sketched cake, haphazard, and the Professor pointed at it with his pencil.

'Think of it as a cake with three layers.'

He pointed at the bottom layer.

'Here is your life – your childhood, your history, the whole maelstrom of life.' He drew messy swirls across the bottom layer to illustrate the maelstrom.

He scratched an arrow between the bottom layer and the middle layer, pausing there with the tip of the pencil.

'The bottom layer feeds into the middle layer, and here in this middle layer we have emotions – anxiety, depression, anger . . . and so on.'

His pencil did a swift arc upwards.

'And these emotions feed into this top layer. This layer is your behaviour – bingeing and vomiting.' He jabbed his pencil into the middle layer of the messy cake. 'This is the level at which the antidepressants work, here at the level of your emotions.'

I nodded, not taking my eyes off the picture he'd drawn.

'And here' – he jabbed at both the first and second layers, the behaviour on top, and the emotion underneath – 'is where Penny will work.'

'Is it CBT?' I asked.

'"CBT" is a very broad term. Yes, Penny will use some cognitive behavioural therapy, but she will also use a number of other methods. I suggest you talk to Penny and arrange to meet her.'

I left with Penny's number and that week, at a quiet end of the large open-plan building at the BBC, I heard Penny's voice over the phone for the first time. I liked her immediately. Her voice was calm. It wasn't a quiet or a loud voice, it wasn't authoritative or tentative, it had a perfect balance. We arranged to meet the following week, to talk.

In my parents' kitchen I drew the cake on the first page of the flipchart and explained what I thought it meant. I explained that the emotions in the middle layer, generated by whatever maelstrom was going on in the bottom layer, resulted in the behaviour in the top. In other words, when I am anxious, depressed, angry, I binge and vomit. I wrote 'B + V' in the top layer, then added a full stop. I explained that Penny was working at the level of my behaviour and also at the level of my emotions, with the help of the weekly blue diaries we keep track of when I binge and vomit, and looking at what emotions and what thinking preceded the binge and vomit. That it always comes from somewhere, that it is always triggered by something. We all looked at the cake I had drawn. It was a relief to be able to look at something concrete.

'It's a good illustration,' Dad said, approvingly.

We all nodded, our eyes still on the cake on the flipchart. The fridge whirred. Two blue tits landed on the feeder outside the window. I wished I had more, I wished I had a chart, or a formula, something that would explain it all, simply, in clear strong lines on the pages of the flipchart, in neat, neutral categories. As a family we are not accustomed to discussing negative feelings. Being Positive is the sacred mantra of us all, handed down from both our parents. It seems like a dark and dangerous place, that world of dark feelings and emotion. I fear that once I stray into that territory I may never be able to find my way back.

I could tell that the three of them were waiting for me to go on, and not for the first time I wished that there was a magic answer, and I harboured even then, when I knew it would never turn out that way, a fervent wish that Penny might extract this magic answer from the chaotic details of my situation, my past, my present, my behaviours. Perhaps the key to all of this was something I hadn't thought of. Perhaps it was something I was not even aware of. I had had a fantasy when I first met Penny that she would present me with this key, triumphantly – hand it over in a velvet-lined box – and then it would all become clear, all fall into place, and I would be free. But I didn't have that answer, not yet, so instead I handed the pen back to my father, who took his place beside the flipchart and extended the pointer.

Four

Sussex. April 2006

'ENVIRONMENTAL FACTORS: BEFORE' has been ambushed by a cake whose meaning leaches away as we stare at it. After a short pause, my father takes hold of the bottom right corner of the page and turns to the next clean page. He removes the top of the pen and writes: 'Factors from Caroline's Childhood'. He underlines this and puts a bullet point underneath it. Then the phone rings. The ring in this house is deafening, pealing through all the rooms and out to the ends of the garden so that my parents can hear it even if they are cutting back the Nepalese rhododendrons that grow rampantly in the acidic soil beyond the house.

My father answers it, still holding the red pen.

'Allen Jones.'

He states his name confidently, simply, just as it is. He has done it this way for as long as I can remember, and I know it will never change.

I used to try to copy my father's manner of answering the

phone when I was at work. I thought it would make me sound practical, confident, straight from the shoulder. But I never mastered the art of keeping the syllables level, with an equal weight of sureness in each one. It would tip up at the end into a question, an invitation, a givingness about it I didn't want to convey but somehow couldn't help. Or it would falter some-where in the middle, the weak 'r' at its heart, exposing some weakness of personality.

'Ah, Richard. What can I do for you?'

It's for Dad. He heads for his study to consult his notebook. There's a moment of quiet after he leaves the room, as though he has taken with him all practicality, all purposefulness, and we sit listening to the ticking clock.

'Shall we have some tea?' Mother says.

She takes the teapot out of the cupboard and boils the kettle. I walk to the full fruit bowl, choose a banana, and eat it leaning against the countertop. Anna leans back against the wooden spindles of the chair. She brushes her fingertips against the hair at her temples. I'm standing behind her and we're both looking at the new title: 'Factors from Caroline's Childhood'. I'm curious to know what my parents consider to be the salient factors from my childhood but I'm also dreading this conversation. I already know I won't get drawn in. This is quicksand territory. This is where I feel it might tip into something approximating Blame. I am not prepared to apportion responsibility elsewhere for where I am now, nor am I even able to lay under scrutiny the external circumstances of our itinerant lives as children. Not here in my parents' kitchen. It would be treachery. I am not prepared to cast shadows across our family history. If they arise I must try to dis-cuss them honestly, but I know I am a coward in this. I don't want to hurt anyone's feelings – and who is to say that my version is true, anyway? Who is entitled to say what is true in any family's history? It is all shades of grey, interpretations and misinterpretations, something that passes one person by might be the thing that tips another onto a different journey; and all, in the end, coloured by imagination and weakened by unreliable memory.

Perhaps the way we tell our family story is true, as true as any other – that we had a privileged childhood in Africa, we travelled to beautiful, remote corners of the earth, attended good schools, had loving, adventurous parents. We spent our holidays swimming in oceans and lakes, camping in game parks and forests. We had geese and dogs and homing pigeons, cats and rabbits and chickens, scavenger fish and neon tetras, which we bought in the shopping centre run by East African Asians in Westlands. We had a creek at the border of our land where a dead baboon gathered flies one dry season. Sykes' monkeys played in our trees. We kept a lookout for rhino on our way to school in the car while we practised our times tables.

I look up at the framed photograph above the kitchen door which reminds us of where we came from. In the yellow African sunlight my brother William, my sister and I stand skinny-legged in the tall grass at the end of our garden, just beyond where the garden met the dirt-track road. William rests his hand on the head of Nimrod the black Labrador, Anna has her arms around our cat, and I stand behind them in blue shorts. In the background two giraffe pass unconcernedly on their way elsewhere. This is our family history.

But we also moved often. Every few years on average, though we were eight years in Kenya. By the time I left for boarding school in England at nearly seventeen we had lived in Ethiopia,

Lesotho, Kenya, Sudan, Kenya a second time, and Pakistan. One year into my two years at boarding school my parents moved again, from Pakistan back to Ethiopia, the country where I was born. In two of those countries war or the threat of hostility closed down our schools and we lost most of our friends, who were evacuated to their homelands and never came back. We weren't Embassy kids – my parents just found smaller, more local schools and we carried on. We never questioned any of this. None of us kids ever did. There was no choice, of course there wasn't. We did it because that was our father's job with the World Food Programme, feeding starving people, feeding refugee populations, moving food from one place to another on ships and lorries and trains and cargo planes, building grain silos, starting development projects and farming schemes; and we, a united family, always followed my father, who himself followed civil wars and famines and the postings from the programme's headquarters in Rome.

I put my banana peel in the bin. I know that my parents must have discussed these 'Factors from Childhood' and I'm embarrassed that they must appear so trivial in the scheme of things. Perhaps last night after we all went to bed they sat up with the murmur of the World Service in the background and talked it through. Or maybe they've been mulling over what went wrong for years, but I just haven't known it.

Mother has set out the teapot and mugs on the table. I notice she doesn't take out the cake that I know is in the bread bin. Usually we have something sweet with our tea, but she must think that leaving the cake safely in its bin is helpful to me. Perhaps it is today. I don't yet know which way the day will swing.

Dad comes back into the kitchen.

'Cup of tea. Lovely. How about a digestive biscuit?'

I take the packet of digestives out of the tin in the fridge and overlap six of them in a circle on a plate. I take one myself, feeling safe. Digestives are from a free, happy period, in Kenya. I used to eat them in the dusty house of my friends, the Twins, after riding their horses. Their dad was the vet and their mum trained racehorses. Later, I envied the Twins because they were real Kenyans. I didn't realise we weren't real ones until after we left and that life closed in on itself, as lives do. I can go back, but not really.

I eat my digestive slowly, dipping it into my tea, watching the patch of dark spreading across its surface as it sucks up the liquid, then biting into it when it's at the perfect state of both soft and crunchy. Kenyan digestives are smaller, thicker and denser than their English relations. They don't fall apart as easily. I think of the Twins. One of them is now a champion jockey in Kenya and gay, with a black Kikuyu girlfriend from the bush; the other is in England, a suburban doctor with long hair and three children. If I had to choose to be one of them, I'd be the champion jockey. I'm the right height. I'd soon get as lean and muscled as the jockey Twin if I wore a heavy backpack and went for long runs along the dusty roads, like Kenyan jockeys do. But then I'd have to be a real Kenyan, which I'm not.

'Shall we carry on?' Dad asks. I sit down next to Anna, but slightly further back from the table. Her thick hair is drawn back, the ends of her dark-brown curls rest on her shoulders.

'Factors from Childhood,' Dad announces. 'Maybe it would be helpful to think about what these were.' He's looking at me. The bullet point hangs unblinkingly at the left of the page.

'I don't know,' I say.

Anna knows I was going to say this, so she says it for me: 'We moved around a lot.' Anna is the one who challenges the Being Positive, when she needs to.

Dad writes 'Moving frequently' on the page.

'Yes, and it was very upsetting, when we left Pakistan, in particular,' Mum adds. 'I'll never forget how upset you were, saying goodbye to Lin in Pakistan.'

Lin. Lin was my best friend then. I was also in love with her. Perhaps that's not so strange, now that I come to think about it. Perhaps all young girls are in love, in lust, in some way with their best friends. It was an intense, angry sort of adolescent love, and powerful. I never wanted to be without her but we fell out all the time over real and imagined slights. We both had boyfriends too and knew without being told and without ever discussing it that we were free to kiss and touch each other's private bodies only after dark and after our friends had fallen asleep at weekend sleepovers. I still remember the first time we held hands, in the dark, in a Land Rover that was travelling back to Islamabad from Peshawar. Lin's dad was in American intelligence, providing arms to the Mujahideen in Afghanistan so they could fight the Russians. They were evacuated when Saddam Hussein invaded Kuwait. She lives in Missouri now, with her girlfriend.

'Hmm. Yes.' I nod. I'm embarrassed at the display of emotion from all those years ago that Mother is referring to. I'm not even sure what particular incident she remembers. I have a memory of crying in the driveway of our house in Islamabad after Lin left but I don't remember anything else – I don't remember saying goodbye, or where we said goodbye, or what we said, or what I did next. But I don't ask Mum about it because I don't want to be drawn into this except on my own terms.

I also have a memory of walking into the dark kitchen in the middle of that night and smashing a bottle of the kind we used to store boiled water. I picked up a shard of glass and cut into my right thumb so blood rose up in a neat line. I don't know if my mother remembers this, if this is what she is referring to. If it weren't for the tiny line of a white scar, I might have forgotten it too. It was minor, really. Mother heard the bottle smash and came into the kitchen. I said it was an accident, but with everything that was going on then I doubt she believed me. She'd have taken my lead and understood – known – that I didn't want to talk about it. She took my hand and rinsed the blood off under the tap.

So, yes, it was hard to say goodbye to Lin – it must have been, but again, it was one of those things. And it was a long time ago. We wrote each other long letters, pages and pages long, for a few years from opposite sides of the world, she from America and I from Pakistan and then boarding school in England, but eventually that dried up, subsumed by everything else that was going on, and by distance, and by falling in love with other people. That life was over. And one day at boarding school, I took out the pile of her letters and looked at them coldly, at the drawings and the jokes and the diagrams that we used to find funny, that used to have meaning in the old days, and I spread the letters over my desk, in the hour between prep and bedtime, with the whoosh of cars driving down the hill into the small characterless town outside my bedroom window, the bedroom on the top floor of a creaking boarding house, which I shared with a girl whose parents were in Ecuador, and I saw that it was all childish and no longer had any meaning, and so I threw all her letters away.

'And it was very hard for you when we moved to Ethiopia when you were at boarding school,' Mum says.

'Yes,' I say. And I feel I need to explain why it was hard; why I found it hard, why I couldn't just take it in my stride, like other people do. 'It was just not knowing where home was,' I say. 'Not really having a home to think of,' I offer.

This I do remember. I remember sitting in the phone booth in the boarding house with my sister, two terms in, and my mother's voice over the long-distance line from Pakistan telling us that we were moving to Ethiopia. Another move, another closing-off of what was left of our familiar life after Saddam Hussein invaded Kuwait and Operation Desert Storm began, and the school closed down for security reasons. But still, Pakistan was my home, was our home, with our house on the residential street in the city that was purpose-built in the sixties to replace Karachi as the capital for the country. With our friends and our dog and our bicycles. With Siddiq, the cook, in the kitchen and Baba-Ji asleep on his charpoy in the driveway. And people working in the blistering heat in the month of Ramadan when they wouldn't touch even a drop of water. And the feeling of celebration and release at the evening call to prayer when the smells of fires and cooking filled the city, and Siddiq would take his first sip of water.

We swam at Khanpur Dam at weekends, and at the Islamabad Club, which I could get to on my bike only if I followed my friend Sanam Majid, who knew the way. There we would drink mango juice and burn in the sun on the edge of the stark, unadorned pool, with the women in shalwar khameez, their clothes billowing and floating on top of the water above them. Then we'd cycle home, parched in the heat, at the end of the sweltering day, to the cool house with its ceiling fans, hoping that Mum was at home, because it never felt right when she wasn't there, and she usually was.

Pakistan was home.

But this time, this move, I was in a boarding school in England, and with our parents moving to Ethiopia it left us nowhere we could picture as home. Certainly not here, in England. I cried that day as my sister and I walked back into the school to lessons, and she hugged me. I buried my head in her shoulder and she put her arms around me. But after that we never spoke about it again.

In my father's concluding notes, which he types up in his study late that evening and slips under my bedroom door, he writes:

Factors from Childhood:
- Our nomadic way of life, living in eight different countries during her lifetime, has constantly disrupted Caroline's relationships.
- The evacuation of all of her American friends from Pakistan in a critical teenage year was traumatic for her, especially the loss of her best friend, Lin.
- In retrospect it seems that Caroline used to hide her emotions, although this was not obvious at the time. She was able to stop herself crying even when Nimrod the black Labrador died.
- Caroline has never been as communicative as her brother and sister. She did not tell her parents that she was going to be head girl at her Kenyan prep school, and we only found out from a friend halfway

through her first term as head girl.

- Caroline was always so good academically and at sports that she was automatically assumed to be doing well and perhaps did not get as much enthusiastic praise and encouragement as her siblings. Her report cards were consistently too good.

- Caroline was not happy at boarding school at nearly 17 but didn't tell. She learned early on how to binge and vomit from another girl at school. She recognises that there were probably good reasons for sending her there, including that she would have finished at her Pakistan school anyway after another year and we were in the process of moving to Ethiopia.

And so in just a short space of time we had dealt with Professor Lacey's grey mass, the messy swirls of the bottom layer, the maelstrom. It had been reduced to a few succinct points by my father's pen.

My parents' home, 1 Ekulu Lane, Enugu, Nigeria. 1970.

PART II:
BOARDING SCHOOL
1991-1993

Handstands at Magadi. Kenya, 1983.

Five

First term at boarding school. England.
November 1991. Sixteen years old

According to the ledger Priya Haria has gone to the shops, N'gillan Faal and Rosie Bain have gone to Knowle Park, and Maissa Karim is in the library.

I pause at the door of the boarding house, skim down the names of the girls who have left the house before me, their names and destinations and time out entered in the signing-out book placed on a music stand by the door. The boarding house is mostly quiet. Dully quiet. It's a Sunday, and I have never known days to drag so slowly as they do here in England, in this boarding school in a quiet, clean commuter town in Kent. I run my fingertips along the string that ties the pen to the book, then enter my name, my destination and the time. Caroline Jones. Town. 1.15 p.m.

I hear the theme tune from *Neighbours* coming from the living-room area. Most girls are away this weekend, visiting guardians or family, but a few stragglers with nowhere to go lounge on the sofas in the common room, ranged around the television set. They're watching the *Neighbours* omnibus in their pyjamas, eating toast, their backs against a bank of Georgian windows that look out onto the neat lawns of the house and a thin grey sky.

Ali Archer, Jess Norrie, Sophie Knight. Point-to-point. One of them has drawn a cartoon smiling face and a star on the entry in the ledger.

They were in high spirits when they left this morning. They are the minority in the house – a handful of English girls to balance out all those who have come from abroad, from India, Nigeria, Korea, Saudi Arabia, Kenya, Germany, to board here. My sister and I have come from Pakistan. That morning the group of English girls had left in a flurry of makeup and excitement on their way to the point-to-point. I was upstairs on the landing when they were putting on their makeup and deciding what to wear in front of the house's one full-length mirror. One of them asked me why I wasn't coming. I'd never heard of a point-to-point and she told me what it was: a sort of horse race across the countryside, with jumps and hounds, perhaps even a fox. I pictured handsome English men with red cheeks and riding-hats leaping over hedgerows, chasing foxes across fields. I caught sight of myself in the mirror, behind the brightness of her turquoise blouse, looking heavy-faced, heavy-haired, in a tent-like top I'd bought from an Afghan trader in the local Friday market in Islamabad, where my sister and I bought all our clothes before we came to England.

The *Neighbours'* jingle merges into muted dialogue. I drop the pen on its piece of string and push open the door into the street. I put my hand in my jeans pocket and curl my fingers around the ten-pound note there, folded into three equal rectangles.

Head down and braced against the wind that whistles up the flagstoned street, I hurry towards the centre of town, straight down the hill on the narrow pavement. I'm at the point where the town splits into two roads and I look up. I'm not thinking about anything, I am deliberately emptied, so when I catch sight of my reflection sliding across the estate agent's window I have no defence. The loose-fitting top I'm wearing to conceal the size of my breasts billows out, making me shapeless and wide. I look away quickly but it's too late. It's there already, my reflection, stuck inside me. I can't get away from it. The thick hair, the big breasts, the formless body, the heavy face, the jeans too big, slipping across the windows of an estate agent in a town somewhere in Kent, which is somewhere south of the M25, which is a circular motorway that surrounds London. I know this. I studied the road atlas, and on a scrap of paper I drew a diagram for my sister. One circle for London: 'This is London.' A bigger circle surrounding it for the M25: 'This is a giant motorway that circles all the way around London.' And then a spindly line running south and east. 'And this is a smaller road than the motorway, an "A road" it's called, that goes to where we are.'

'How do you know that?' she asked me.

'I looked at the road atlas.'

We're in a part of the world known as the Medway. We've studied the Medway in our geography lessons, but still, I'm not sure what it is. I know that I don't like it. It is grey and cold and has no smell to it, no fire or smoke or tree smell, no smell of heat easing off as the time for prayer begins in the yellow and purple-brown evening sky of Islamabad, no smell of Siddiq or his cooking, Siddiq in his shalwar khameez with the stained teacloth over his shoulder and his chickenpoxed skin, rolling out pasta in sheets on the floured kitchen table. No smell of my mother, at home.

And now that I have caught sight of my reflection in a shop window it has frozen me here in the Medway. I can no longer be empty.

I hurry on, keeping my eyes on my shoes until I'm at the traffic lights. Here there's an island of shops and restaurants at the end of which is a wedge-shaped teashop called Coffee Call. I peer through its window at the carrot cake. Someone in my house, the International House, was recently given a whole carrot cake from Coffee Call by a parent on her birthday and she shared it out amongst all of us. Thick cream-cheese icing. Wet inside, substantial, delicious. Ever since, I have fantasised about picking up a whole cake and scrunching into it, the way I used to fantasise as a child about scrunching into a whole roast boar like Obelix at the feast at the end of the *Asterix* comic books. When my mother drove my sister and me back to school after half-term before she went back to rejoin our father in Pakistan just a few weeks ago, I sat in the back and stared out of the car window at the dark British night, feeling besieged by the hostile lights on the motorway and the rain on the windscreen, and so I lost myself in a fantasy of eating this carrot cake, eating all of it, then starting a second one.

But Coffee Call cakes are expensive, and I need to spend my pocket money wisely. It has to last more than just today. I tear myself away from the window, my mouth filled with saliva, and the image of my ugly reflection in the estate agent's window obliterated by an orgy of cake fantasy.

I return to the traffic lights, recross the road, and continue downhill to the supermarket. Its clean glass doors slide open to me. The first aisle on the right-hand side is the chocolate aisle. I stand, rows and rows of chocolate before me, paralysed. I am alone. There is only me. I can choose whichever bar I like, as big as I like.

And there in the middle of the shelves is a giant bar of white chocolate. To me, it is even more exotic than brown chocolate, even creamier and sweeter. The Milky Bar gleams at me. It is beautiful. I pick it off the shelf and hold it in my hand, feeling the weight of it. It's a giant bar. Enough for a whole family. Can I really buy this just for myself? Can I eat this whole thing all myself, and not have to share it with anybody? Yes, I can. Nobody will even have to know. It will be my indulgence, for me only. I walk to the cash register and place it down on the dark rubber of the conveyor belt. I watch it as it is pulled along towards the attendant. Yes, I can have it. Yes, it is mine. I can buy this, there's nobody to stop me. Nobody, even, to witness this greed.

White chocolate did not exist at all in East Africa, nor in Pakistan. It isn't like the chocolate bar we were allowed as our weekly treat at the swimming pool in Kenya. I would fill in the chit carefully, leaning over the wooden bar in my wet costume, trying not to drip onto the paper: in the first column 'Cadbury's Crunch'. Next row down, first column: 'Dairy Milk', for Anna. I would write my signature at the bottom of the chit, then examine it critically. It was never as good as the signatures we practised on our friends' blackboard, but I couldn't have a second try.

The four-square by four-square chocolate bars Bethwell, the barman, handed over to us were produced in a Cadbury's factory in Nairobi – we knew that from the wrapper. '*Asante sana* Bethwell!' Anna would shout as she slipped off her stool and ran back to our spot by the diving board, leaving a puddle of water where she'd sat. We'd join our friends there and lie on our stomachs on the hot flagstones, heads together in the middle, legs pointing out of the circle, toes resting lightly on the burning concrete, the water trapped beneath our costumes warm and sticky and smelling of baked dust. We'd unwrap the bars carefully and place them on top of their silver foil, face up, ignoring our friends with their sun-browned arms and hair green from the pool's chlorine, fighting to be the next to leap from the end of the diving board, and Daphne Mutisa practising handstands in the shallow end, with water beading off her African hair when she burst up for air.

I'd cross my arms, rest my chin on my forearms and watch the chocolate's edges soften in the sun. After just a few minutes it would have melted, but it retained its perfect chocolate bar shape. A slight lightening of the colour, a softening of the contours, but to anyone else it still looked like a normal bar of chocolate.

'Is it ready?' I'd ask Anna. She's good at judging things like this.

She dips a finger into a square and a fold of chocolate skin sticks to her fingertip. It's ready. We'd eat slowly, one fingertip at a time, and when it was gone, we'd suck the last smudges of chocolate from its silvery folds. Then we'd leap up to join the fight for a place at the end of the diving board, eager to show off our one-and-a-half-twist somersault that Dad taught us, the chocolate bar forgotten until the following week when we would be allowed another. Until then we wouldn't give it another moment's thought.

But here, in this town, I can buy this bar, this giant bar, and tomorrow I can buy another, if I want to, with what remains of my ten pounds. This act is invisible to anyone else. There is nobody to see, nobody even to check the chits at the end of each month. Mother, straight-backed at the dining-room table, a red wavy skirt reaching to the middle of her brown calves, her ankles crossed, her forearms resting softly on the tabletop as she checks the pile of chits, one at a time, licking her index finger before she flicks to the next, unhurried, easy. They always add up, the chits, and if they don't she knows it is no more than a simple mistake.

I hurry up the hill, back to the boarding house, making sure to watch my shoes so I don't get caught in the shop windows.

When I arrive at the house I take the back way in, past the laundry rooms. I see Clara, the quiet English girl with slight shoulders and pale skin and strange allergies, her back to the window, waiting for the last spin of the washing machine to finish. She is watching the spinning drum. I wonder if she too has become aware of time here. I'd never thought of it before, of how it passes, or doesn't pass, or how it can go so slowly, like this. So slow and unformed and empty that it makes you want to break something. I don't stop to talk to her. The chocolate bar in the plastic bag I'm gripping makes a mockery of the spinning drum, the girls watching *Neighbours*. It fills all the empty spaces in between. I walk through the small kitchen. Priya Haria is back from the shops. She's melting Mars Bars in the microwave. I climb the steps to the top of the house, to the small bedroom I share with a roommate whose parents are in Ecuador. She has gone to visit her brother in London. I shut the door, sit on the bed, take off my shoes, remove the Milky Bar from its bag, lay it on the bed, unwrap it carefully and sit cross-legged before it. It lies naked and white in front of me. I undo the top button of my jeans. I eat, at first one square at a time, then I break off whole rows of six squares and gobble them up, with the hum of traffic pouring into this Kent town from elsewhere outside my window.

Six

First holiday from boarding school.
Sri Lanka. Easter, 1992

We climb out of the car, straighten ourselves, brushing airport smells from our clothes, squinting against the bright sunshine. We have finally arrived. Anna and I have flown, at the end of the second term, from England to Pakistan, where we joined our parents to travel to Sri Lanka, and here we will spend our Easter holiday.

We look around us from our spot under a cluster of palm trees. Painted fishermen's boats tilt sideways on the sand, still, in the heat of midday. Here in the south of the island the sea is treacherous, as the beach shelves sharply at the point where huge waves crash in from the Indian Ocean. There is no one about, no fishermen. They must be taking refuge from the heat.

There's a faint scratching sound, the rustle of dry leaves, and Anna and I look down at the same time. Under the nearest palm a turquoise-tailed lizard stares at us, lifting his neat green head up and down, up and down; then he loses his nerve and scatters away over cracked-open husks of coconuts and the spindly shadows cast by the palms.

I glance at Anna. She looks pale, her clothes too warm, too thick, for this climate. She looks different here, her face a little rounder, her eyebrows darker, her thick curling hair, pulled back by a rubber band, darker too. It's as though I haven't really paid her any attention, haven't really seen her, these past months at school. It's as though the light in England isn't really good for seeing things properly. We laugh at the lizard; it has stopped a safe distance away and is watching us, its head bobbing up and down.

Spread out under the trees is a string of simple wooden cabins. Anna and I will share ours. We go in and she drops her bag on one of the narrow single beds and pulls on her costume. We will swim before we do anything else. I know that the sea will make me feel more a part of this, make both of us feel more a part of this. This is where we belong, after all. Not here, in Hikkaduwa, not here specifically, but here in this heat, in a place where there are lizards with turquoise tails and a background chorus of insects. I sit on the other bed and look around the room. We have mosquito nets, dangling in loose knots over the beds, a long mirror propped against one wall, a bamboo cupboard, a desk. Nothing more than that, and this simple, unwavering heat.

Anna is ready.

'Shall I wait for you, Sis?' she asks.

'No, I'm just coming,' I say.

She pulls a *kikoy*, a length of Kenyan cloth, self-consciously around her midriff, and leaves. I watch through the window as she catches up with our parents and they stand looking out to sea, then walk arm in arm along the beach, the three of them together. The wide sandy beach curves away from them into the far distance. They pause and look back, waiting for me to join them. They walk into the shallow surf. The waves crash onto the beach.

I draw down the blinds against the bright light, and pick up my bikini, examine it briefly, then place it back on the bed. Shafts of slanting sunshine still penetrate the cabin between the slats of the blind. With my back turned against the room I pull off my clothes quickly and step first into the bikini bottoms, then pull the top piece over my head. Still without turning to the mirror I adjust my breasts, pulling and tucking them into place, kneading them into the flimsy triangles of black material that seem too small against my skin. Then I draw in my breath and turn to the long mirror.

I scan my body up and down, pausing at my stomach and breasts. I am striped by the light that falls through the blinds. I breathe in, turn sideways, and watch myself in profile, my mouth set. I straighten, twist my long hair into a knot and remain standing there, one hand holding the knot at the base of my neck, critical. There's too much of me. Large breasts, small bottom, not enough of a waist, thin legs. I exhale, look away from the mirror, absently raise my right arm into a beam of light and rotate it back and forth in a tunnel of slowly moving motes of dust, transfixed by the whiteness of my skin. The hairs on my arm catch the light but do not shine. They are no longer blonde but a dull brown. In just one winter, my first in England, my arm has turned a colour I don't recognise; I don't think I belong to this colour, but it will change. I shift back to face myself in the mirror, gather with both hands a fold of soft flesh above my pubic bone and pinch it hard with spread fingers. As I release it, red marks appear. Then I lay my palms flat against my breasts and push against them, flattening them. Again I turn sideways and watch myself in the mirror. I wish I did not have these breasts. Without them I could be more like Emmanuelle Béart. I remember a scene from *Manon des Sources* in which she dances naked by a waterfall, tiny-breasted, beautiful, wild. I could never dance naked, like she can; it would look ridiculous, my breasts are too big. They would swing around uncontrolled and heavy. I regard myself cruelly in the mirror.

'I am fat,' I think, and am filled with hate.

I think of the pound cake I ate on the flight from Pakistan to Sri Lanka that morning. The stewardess with the veil over her dark hair and her green angular uniform had handed out thick slices of yellow pound cake in plastic wrappers alongside the cups of tea. My father and I had sat happily side by side, eating our cake and looking out at the subcontinent's changing landscapes, talking about the different countries we were flying over on our journey to the island, where we are to meet my brother and his girlfriend, Laura, who are travelling there on a motorbike. On the plane Dad gave up his window seat for me, and we leaned together towards the window.

'Those mountains' – Dad pointed to a range to the west of us in the Hindu Kush, we could just see their glinting peaks – 'are in Afghanistan. Just over there, of course' – he used his forefinger to make a curve in the air, to indicate the other side of the mountains – 'the Mujahideen are fighting the Russians.' I know this. The Soviets are fighting the Mujahideen because they want Afghanistan to be their ally in the Cold War, but the Mujahideen don't want this. I know what they look like, the

Mujahideen: they look like the pale-skinned Afghans in the local markets of Islamabad, selling clothes and carpets. They wear loose-fitting clothes and flat hats that roll up around the edges, and they carry Kalashnikovs. We wear those hats too, in Islamabad, during the cold winters. I don't know what the Russians look like, though. The Russians will never win, Dad says. The Mujahideen are waging a guerrilla war against them, supported by billions of dollars from the United States and weapons too, and nobody knows the land, the mountains, the valleys, the hiding places like the Mujahideen. The Russians must feel very far from home.

'Where are all the refugees?' I asked. I know there are three million of them down there, somewhere. I imagine we should be able to see them, even from here.

'Down there. You know, towards Quetta, and D. I. Khan, where we drove last summer, all along that border region, in camps. Those are the mountains they had to cross to get to Pakistan.'

Then we banked away from the Himalayas and flew southwards towards India, high over the Indus River and its orderly irrigation canals built by the British, just a speck of plane glinting over the empty Thar Desert.

Now I look in the mirror and I hate myself for eating the yellow cake. I shouldn't have eaten it. Then I wouldn't be so fat. I squeeze the bulge of fat on my stomach again, with more venom, leaving more angry red marks. It's not good enough. It's pathetic.

I hear my name called from the beach; it seems to come from very far away. The sun shines, unrelenting, between the slats.

It is clear that Dad thinks my sister and I are overweight. He does not make this obvious at first, but I imagine his eyes follow me, follow both of us, critically, when we run into the sea that first day. The next morning, over a breakfast of toast and slices of papaya, he suggests it's a good idea for us all to avoid eating lunch – we should eat breakfast, he says, then a good meal in the evening. By the end of the holiday we will all be fit and healthy. Dad is right; Anna and I know it, Mum knows it too. We will feel better if we are fitter and leaner.

A starling hops up onto the wooden balcony, takes three quick sideways jumps, eyeing the toast, then hops away. I look at my plate. Half a piece of toast, the butter melted into it. I feel a fleeting thrill at the prospect that by the end of this holiday I will be leaner, harder, better. In a spirit of optimism, and a shared family instinct for self-improvement, we all agree to the plan.

After breakfast Anna and I walk onto the beach and watch the waves, waiting for a lull in their fierceness so that we can run into the sea. The tide here is strong, so we can't swim too far out from the shore. We know how to dive under the waves so that they don't hurl us back onto the beach. The waves crash and crash again, then still for a moment, and we run in, shouting. After the swim we wash off the sand and lie on our single beds in dry *kikoys*, to read. I am hungry. It is not yet noon. An immovable hunger sets in. By the evening I fall on my food, ravenous, never satisfied.

Dad took a picture of me on the beach. I'm in profile, standing on the sand looking out to sea at some distance from his lens. One evening after we return to our home in Islamabad, and just a few days before Anna and I return to our English boarding school, Dad arranges the slides in the projector and we gather together in the living room. Our dog, a German Shepherd called Bhuna, sits next to Dad.

We switch off the lights and listen to the projector as it whirs and clicks, the ceiling fan flicking shadows into the garden. The garden here is no more than a well-tended square of grass surrounded by walls, a few fragrant bushes with flowers, and a mango tree in the corner.

The slides slot into place one by one. Sri Lanka, the waves, my brother and his girlfriend running into the sea.

Odd verses of Siddiq's strange operatic singing come to us from behind the swing door of the kitchen as he sweats over the frying chillies and turmeric, wiping at his pock-marked face with the teacloth he always carries over his shoulder.

Dad pauses when the slide he took of me comes up against the wide white screen. I have not seen it before. I look huge in it. Much bigger, surely, than I really am. I am leaning slightly forward, lost in thought, hands on my hips, pushing at something in the sand with my toe. I am not aware of the lens.

'Dad,' I say, angrily, 'I really don't like that picture.'

Dad laughs, as though the slide is meant to be a joke.

'I suppose it isn't very flattering,' he says.

I know then that he has voiced this to himself before, perhaps as he slotted the transparencies into their ridges. I know that he deliberately chose this slide, as a lesson. The next one drops into place. I feel Anna's sympathy in the room full of evening shadows, the fan flicking over us.

Slap, slap, slap, the sound of Baba-Ji, our elderly chowkidar, slapping chapattis in the kitchen behind the swing door; he is as soft and as quiet as Siddiq is loud.

The image is replaced on the wall by one of my brother and Laura on their motorbike, happy, brown, thin. Free. They are free because they are thin, I understand that now. They are not weighed down in their bulk, ungainly. I covet their thinness and their freedom. The slides continue but I do not move on; I feel bitter, ungrounded. I am wounded by my father's image of me.

And yet I know what he is saying is true, of course I do. I can't react. I daren't say more. I do not want to appear over-sensitive by reacting more strongly, by bringing it up again in anger when we have already moved on, when there are other, more important, things. We don't do that kind of thing, in this family. And I know that the slide is a lesson in another sense: my reaction to it is a test of my resistance to self-pity. After all, fatness is a simple formula. Dad pointed this out on our holiday, but it isn't the first time I've heard him say it: If you take in more than you burn off, you gain weight. It's as simple as that. Yes, it's as simple as that.

Now the smell of frying mince. We will eat Siddiq's keema curry with Baba's chapattis, with raita and rice and chunks of green lime pickle, and the boiled water stored in the glass bottles. Siddiq has stopped singing and is saying something to Baba. Baba's soft voice, Siddiq's strong voice, Siddiq's laughter. Dad rolls up the screen. I walk out onto the veranda and look at the mango tree in the dusky evening light. Two crows sit on the wall by the gate. The call to prayer begins, calling to us over the tin gate, rolling and building as it spins in the air around the house. The evening sky always looks more beautiful, more mysterious and sacred during the call to prayer. The crows fly away.

Bhuna flops onto the tiled floor next to me, panting in the heat. She is a de-mining dog, trained in Thailand to sniff out landmines in Cambodia after the war there, and then transported to Pakistan to do the same on the Afghan border. I reach down and scratch behind her ears. When she retired she came to us with a booklet of commands. Dad practises them outside on the roadside, standing straight-backed and proud at the end of this quiet city street with its spaced-out houses behind their tin gates, interspersed with fields of wild marijuana. He calls out commands in Thai while the old dog runs up and down the road, low on her back haunches, sweeping imaginary landmines from the neighbourhood.

Anna and I return to England for the third term of boarding school. Mum is tearful; Dad stands next to her, smiling proudly at us as we walk away. I turn around for one last look and they are both still waving, Dad is squeezing Mum's arm, comforting her. The two of them in a sea of Pakistani families with oversized suitcases, saying goodbye, clutching tissues, handing over tiffin tins full of food. Anna is crying, but I am not. The house will feel so empty when we've gone, Mum said. The tall ceilings and the fans blowing the hot air around, and the mangoes ripening on the tree in the front courtyard. Mum won't change the sheets on our beds for a long time; she'll leave them as they are, so she can still smell us there.

As the plane descends into England the following morning we hardly see the ground before we bump down to land. Cloud hangs low over the airport, the grey rain drives down at an angle and splashes feebly back up again off the tarmac, pooling in black puddles. I watch out of the window as a man in a waterproof uniform, in high rubber boots, waves in the aircraft in the rain. I don't like the way this makes me feel, the man in the rain, his arms up, down, up, down; it feels like self-pity. I freeze it there. There is a part of myself I cannot afford to enter, I don't want to enter, a sore, anemone part of myself, so I will avoid it. And I will not let on about it; nobody need know.

Anna, beside me, looks out of the window too. I don't know what she is thinking, but I don't ask. Anna is OK at school, I know that. She likes it in an even, level kind of a way. She has friends, she knows her way around, she knows where she is meant to be when.

The plane rocks gently to a standstill and the lights flicker off as the engine dies. I alone can improve things. If I am fat, it is my fault, of course it is. If I struggle at boarding school, it too is my fault, my responsibility. The man in the rain lowers his arms to his side. Why should it make me feel this way, this man in the rain, as though something is draining out from me, as though the rain is not outside me, but has come inside me, raining from a cavity under my ribs, raining into my stomach. I will overcome it. I will crush it down, if that is what I need to do. From now on these matters are my private domain, where nobody else is permitted to enter.

Seven

Third term at boarding school.
England. May 1992

I learned my behaviour from Frieda. She was a beautiful, plump, dark-haired, blue-eyed girl in the same boarding house. Like mine, her parents were overseas. I remember her sitting one evening, in the half-hour between the end of prep and lights-off, on the side of her bed in the room that she shared with three other girls on the first floor. Hitching up the grey school uniform she wore as short as possible to show off her long legs, she bent over and opened the drawer beneath the bed. She held out a pair of frilly knickers for my inspection. They were white with a pink detail running through the silk edging. They looked expensive and French and delicate.

She told me that her mother had bought them for her one size too small, as an incentive for her to lose weight. She giggled conspiratorially when she told me this, her blue eyes twinkling between dark lashes thick with mascara. It intrigued me that a mother and daughter could have that kind of relationship – it seemed so intimate, so personal. My mother would never do a thing like that, manipulate me in that way. But Frieda's parents were different. In my imagination Frieda's parents lived in a tall townhouse in the centre of a sophisticated European capital; her mother, from what she told me, was glamorous and fashionable, her father I imagined to be a successful businessman.

Frieda and I were sitting at the table in the small kitchen of the annexe to the main boarding house, where we lived. It was morning break after the third lesson. Most of the girls were crammed into the kitchen in an orgy of panicked feasting. A crowd of grey skirts and white shirts and ties were elbowing one other around the industrial toasters, and the family-sized block of Cheddar cheese, the size of a loaf of bread, sat on its cellophane wrapper with knives protruding from it. Giant pots of chocolate spread and a plastic bucket of strawberry jam sat open on the laminate counters next to packs of butter softening under greasy wrappers. We talked between shovelling in the toast as quickly as possible before the bell rang for end of break. The daily tin of biscuits was open on the table, ravaged. All the best ones were gone. The plain, sandy biscuits with a top layer of hard pink sugar coating, always the last to be chosen, sat alone in the tin. The bourbons, the custard creams, the round ones covered in chocolate with the hole in the middle, the ridged shortcakes – biscuits we had never seen at home but here were as common as the blackbirds hopping about in the trimmed hedges that lined the house lawn – had all gone. Even the biscuits with hard flecks of raisins in them had gone.

We'd arrived at the kitchen shortly after the bell and were already halfway through a first round as other girls vied for space at the toaster. I lifted my second slice to my mouth and tore off a large chunk, the butter dribbling down my fingers. I was already thinking about what to have on my next round. Maybe I'd forgo the scramble at the toaster and just spread a couple of large dollops of chocolate spread between two slices of thin white bread. Opposite me, Frieda lifted her toast, smothered in melted butter with sugar melting in pools on its surface, to her plump lips, and we caught one another's eye. We laughed guiltily.

The bell rang. Plates and knives crashed into the sink and the girls fled the kitchen, seizing books and pencil cases, balancing toast on fingertips, tucking in the flaps of their white shirts. As I made for the door, pulling awkwardly at my tights which had begun to sag around my knees, I snatched up the last biscuit, the one with the hard coating. I didn't like this biscuit, especially if I couldn't soften it in tea, but it was better than nothing. I ran behind Frieda, bounding before me, gazelle-legged in her short grey skirt.

That night, back in the kitchen, during the short break between homework sessions, we gathered again to gossip and eat toast. A new tin of biscuits was procured from a locked cupboard by the week's designated break prefect, and again within minutes all that was left was a column of the hard pink ones. I stood in the doorway that evening, the one that connected the kitchen to the main body of the house, hovering slightly on the outside of things and struggling against a desire to toast another round of bread.

That's when Frieda told me her secret. She told me I shouldn't let a fear of getting fat stop me eating what I wanted. There was a way around it. If she wanted to eat lots of toast, she said, she would simply stick her fingers down her throat and make herself sick afterwards, then it was as if she hadn't eaten anything. That way she wouldn't gain weight. I was stunned by what she said. I'd heard once before about this kind of thing. It was from an American girl who was visiting her younger cousin in Pakistan. She was older than us. She told us she had once suffered from an illness called 'bulimia'. But she was so different, this girl. She lived in America. She had a tattoo and dyed hair and though she was only five years older than us she seemed light years older. I hadn't really listened to what she was saying; it was so far removed from anything that concerned me. But what Frieda was telling me was different. This was just vomiting. I had never even thought of it before. So maybe it wasn't as simple a formula as it seemed, Dad's notion about what you take in and what you expend in energy. Maybe this was a way of subverting that limiting law of nature. I wanted to give it a go. Frieda took me under her wing.

She told me it was easier to vomit if you ate a lot, her red pout forming a pretty 'o' around the word. And it was a good idea to drink tea at the same time, to soften it all up inside. So I did. I ate four more pieces of buttered toast with sugar, dipped all four hard biscuits into a cup of tea, drank a glass of milk for good measure and followed her out into the dark, to a bank of toilets outside the house. I went into one stall, Frieda went into the next one, and she called out advice through the partition. I bent over the cold toilet seat, gagging with the feeling of my fingers in my throat, and calling out to ask her if you were supposed to hold down the wiggly bit at the back of the throat, or lift it up to trigger the vomiting. She wasn't sure. I heard her shuffling about in the stall next to mine, checking.

'Try holding it down,' she called out.

I held it down. It wasn't a success that first time. Not much came out, so I wasn't yet convinced that it really could work. It hurt. I didn't like my face being so close to the toilet bowl. What if some of the toilet water, or the vomit, splashed back out again? I felt disappointed. I regretted eating the tower of hard-topped biscuits. I'd have to deal with eating the same way other people did – with self-discipline and restraint. I might have known that there was no way around it.

But I'd try again. Maybe it simply took practice. As the bell rang to signal the beginning of the second homework session I quickly gave it one more go. My eyes watered as I bent over the seat one more time, gagging, trying to coax out the toast I'd just eaten. It came out in hard little lumps.

Eight

Third term at boarding school.
England. July 1992

Mary and Jean are waiting to talk to Matron, who hasn't arrived. Mary is soft, with plump breasts under her apron. Though she is often outside smoking with Jean, she doesn't share Jean's smoker's pallor. Jean appears indifferent to the girls of the International House, but Mary takes an interest in their affairs. Perhaps it's simply that Jean has been there longer, has seen the international girls arrive at the beginning of the sixth form and leave two short years later, scattering back to where they came from and leaving little lasting impact either on the life of the school or on the life Jean lives outside. Mary leans in the doorway separating the kitchen and the hallway that leads to the long-distance telephone and Matron's office. Jean has a bucket in her right hand. Mary and Jean are here to complain to Matron about the state of the toilets.

I pause in the kitchen to talk to the cleaners. I have to get past them to get to my room at the top of the house, but I'll stay here a while as I have nothing in particular to do, and I like talking to Mary. I rest my hockey stick against my naked thigh between my short blue pleated skirt and long red socks that come up to the knee, pull the hem of my red-and-white striped hockey jumper over the ends of my fingers, cross my arms against my chest and tuck my fingers under my armpits to warm them. We played a match on the freezing upper pitch and I didn't play well. I used to love playing hockey in Kenya, and in Pakistan's heat, and I was good at it. I loved the thirst I had after running and running on the dried-out grass of the pitches. Lin and I would race with the rest of the players, our Pakistani opponents' shalwar khameez flapping against them, to the water coolers by the low changing rooms and gulp down water from conical paper cups. But I've lost something here. I don't know what it is. I feel angry on the green grass, angry with the long-legged English girls with their smiles and red cheeks and natural camaraderie, their ease. Angry with the hockey teacher with her short curly hair and strong legs, who watches me with suspicion. I can't control the balls I hit, my stick swings too high, I'm tackling dangerously. I've forgotten how to stop the ball, it slips under the curved head of my stick, and I feel stuck, I can't seem to move to get it back. My timing has gone, my fluidity.

After the game we have tea in the hall, a special tea the sports teams get after matches, with platters of jam doughnuts and sandwiches. The parents of the English kids, the day-boarders, who are allowed to go home at the end of each day, sit with them at long tables, and after tea is over they get into their cars in the car park by the art room and drive away. I eat three jam doughnuts. We're only meant to have one, but there are so many of them there. I notice that some of the girls don't even look at them, but while I'm in the hall it's all I can think about, the platters and platters of doughnuts on the tables, leaking red jam. The English girls go home, the boarders disperse back into the school and I come back to the International House.

'Even your toilets at the top are sometimes blocked with vomit,' Mary confides in me. 'They think they've cleaned it up but they always miss a bit right under the rim, so we know they've been doing it. You can always tell.'

Jean interrupts. 'Shall we wait or shall we go and have a fag first?' she asks Mary.

'Let's wait,' Mary says. Jean's fingers are on the fag packet in her pocket.

'And there's the smell,' Mary goes on.

I know neither of them thinks it's me. Why would they? I'm probably a picture of health. I am normal and sociable. But I feel a tremor of guilt. I share the toilets at the top of the house with my roommate and with the two girls who share the neighbouring room – a rosy, straightforward English girl who plays the clarinet, and a more reticent Korean. Frieda is on the first floor, so I know she is the cause of some of the cleaners' extra work, and I know there are others doing it here and there. We don't talk about it. I don't even talk about it with Frieda. Once you've learnt it, you just get on with it. There's nothing to say. I've become better at it. I do it every now and then, not every day. I often seem to do it at the weekends. Perhaps that's because I have more time then, and nothing in particular to fill it with; and then there's the strange leaking-out feeling that comes back more strongly at weekends.

But I always feel guilty. I know it's wrong; it's not as simple as it sounded, as just being able to eat what you like, and I'm going to stop it soon. I won't do it next term, after the summer holidays. In the meantime I'll make sure to clean up better, under the toilet rim.

Jean starts tapping on her fag packet.

'It's Clara,' Mary says, leaning towards me. Jean nods.

'Clara,' Jean concurs. 'She goes up to there in case we catch her at it on her own floor.'

I can see why the cleaners think it's Clara. Clara's head looks oversized, precarious on her slight body. Her face is round and swollen and she has bad skin. Clara has allergies. Her allergies mean she doesn't have to go to the cafeteria like the rest of us. When we come back from sausages and chips, she's there at the table, in some separate space of her own making, picking at a thin piece of rye and dark, dry foods I've never seen before. Clara is gentle, and still. It seems to me she doesn't like to take up space around her. I like Clara, but I let her take the blame.

Just as Jean is about to lose patience with Mary, Matron arrives still holding her car keys, carrying her giant breasts in front of her. We stand sideways so she can squeeze her body past us to get to her office. It's the room before the booth with the telephone where my sister and I have our long-distance phone calls with our parents. Matron greets us all cheerily. She's twice the size of any of us – hers are definitely the biggest bosoms I've ever seen. She's solid, too; her amplitude strains against her white uniform. She dyes her hair a fake blonde colour. In the summer, Matron invites all the International House girls to her garden. She lets the smokers have a fag by the plastic kiddies' slide, while her husband tends the barbecue. I suppose he must like her having such enormous breasts.

The cleaners start their story for Matron, and I am temporarily forgotten. I pick up my hockey stick and stare idly at the curved end. I listen to Mary and Jean filling Matron in on the state of the toilets. They lean into her doorway, smelling of cigarettes, human under their cleaners' aprons, while Matron, in charge of getting in the food supplies for the house and looking after the welfare of its fifty girls, sits at her desk and listens sympathetically, tutting, shaking her head. Then she takes a tin of biscuits which she keeps on the shelf above her desk and unwraps the plastic seal in one practised move, offers around the consolatory biscuits. Jean takes her packet of cigarettes out of her pocket. Mary and I both take a biscuit.

'Are you ready for your summer holidays?' Matron smiles at me, changing the subject.

'Yes, I can't wait.' This isn't really true. I'm not sure where I'm going.

'Where are you going?' asks Mary.

I cover my mouth with my hand so I can answer while I swallow.

'Ethiopia.'

'I thought you lived in India,' Jean says.

'Pakistan. We used to live in Pakistan. We've just moved. To Ethiopia.'

'Ethiopia?' asks Jean. She doesn't look comfortable with this country. If it weren't for the fact that the house is full of girls from strange places I'd think she didn't believe me. 'What's it like in Ethiopia?' She places emphasis on the 'o'.

'I haven't been since I was born. But it's a beautiful country,'

I say dutifully. 'It isn't what you'd imagine from the TV. It isn't all famine, that's just around the edges. The interior of the country is very fertile and green.'

I know this from my parents. They have always loved Ethiopia even though they were there, the first time around, at a turbulent time in its history. Just before my birth Haile Selassie, the Emperor, was overthrown, and from our house they heard the gunning down of 'the Sixty', when sixty prisoners – ministers and academics and others faithful to the Emperor – were lined up in their prison and shot dead. My mother went into labour soon afterwards, and I was born in the living room of one of the few remaining doctors. My mother said that I was induced early because the doctors were due to go away so had to deliver me quickly. While they ate their evening meal at a table in the front room, she said, the crowds of people needing their attention overflowed from their living room and through the front door, in a line that stretched into the garden and onto the street, all waiting for the doctors to finish eating so they could be seen.

What do I know of Ethiopia? I know that Ethiopians are dignified, beautiful people – I know this from our photograph albums – and they come from a rich and ancient Christian civilisation. There are rock churches, hewn out of mountainsides and Rift Valley lakes. Ethiopian crosses have always hung on the walls of our home, and religious iconic oil paintings by a woman called Madame Goshu. My parents reminisce about the wonderful food – large sour pancakes called *njera* onto which are poured different spiced stews called *wat,* a yoghurt called *aib* and a raw meat called *ketfo.* You tear off the pancake with your right hand and scoop up the sauce. The host usually gathers up the best bits on the plate into a *gursha*, which they place in their guest's mouth, an act of friendship.

My parents had horses in Addis Ababa; they rode out into the hills every morning with my Hindu godfather Brigadier Nambiar, as the cool mists rose over fields of meskel flowers. One horse was so big he was called Samson. And then there were Mulu, Marta and Wolde, who looked after us when we were young. And of course Ethiopia is in Africa, back in East Africa, where we belong.

Anna will go out there before me, because she finishes her final exams before the end of term. It might rain, Mother warned us. Summer in England is the long rains in the highlands of Ethiopia.

'I'm sure you'll have a lovely time,' says Matron.

She opens the biscuit tin again, offers it to Mary and Jean. Offers it to me. Matron's biscuit tins contain all of our break-time biscuits, but a few special ones too. Hers are a deluxe version of our biscuit tins. Some are completely enrobed in chocolate and wrapped in shiny foil.

'Have another,' Matron says.

Nine

Summer holidays from boarding school.
Addis Ababa, Ethiopia. August 1992

The city is awash with mud. Water runs down the windows of the four-wheel drive and turns the city wobbly and imprecise. People crowd under bus shelters and the rain pours off their corrugated tin roofs into rivers of brown rainwater running along the gutters. It doesn't look like much, Addis Ababa. It doesn't look like the old black and white photographs in our photo albums, with beautiful women in white dresses. It is brown.

'This is the main road that runs through the centre of Addis,' Dad says. 'All these buildings here are the various ministries.' He points to standard-issue African government buildings, nondescript square hulks on either side of the road. 'They haven't done well these past years, in fact they look worse now than when we were last here nearly twenty years ago. It all looks communist-era, but it's early days and it's changing. Things are picking up now, now that Mengistu has gone. They say that Zenawi, the new Ethiopian president, is part of a new era of African leader, like Museveni in Uganda. We'll see. Things can't get much worse than they were under the Derg and Mengistu.'

The Derg were the communist military junta who deposed the Emperor one month before I was born, in 1974, and took control of the country. Mengistu, who emerged as the leader of the Derg after finishing off his opponents, has been in power ever since then, up until a few months ago. He imposed his own version of socialism on Ethiopia in a reign known as the Red Terror. He killed hundreds of thousands of people, ordinary people: doctors and teachers and academics and students and peasants, as well as his political enemies. He has gone now; he escaped to Zimbabwe.

We're approaching a set of traffic lights. At the lights two boys in rags and a man with stumps for legs, wheeling himself along on a wooden trolley, compete to get to the windows first. They gather at my father's window, clamouring. I realise they recognise Dad, and his car, its huge radio antenna swinging in front like a giant locust, with 'World Food Programme' and its blue logo: a hand holding a bunch of maize painted across the side of the car.

'Leprosy,' Mum says.

The man's legs and arms end at the joint where his knees and elbows once were, and he has holes where his nose used to be. I get a brief, pitiful look from him. He holds out one of his arm stumps towards me and gestures with his long-ago hand for alms, but he knows where the coins will come from and turns again to my father, suddenly still, while Dad winds the window down and takes a few coins he keeps in the well between the driver and passenger seats.

I see the edge of my father's ironed lightweight shirt and his strong brown arm extend a coin out to the muddied stump of the beggar's arm. Rain trickles into the holes where his nose was. The beggar drops the coin into the trolley from the end of his stump, then bows his head and touches his forehead in thanks.

'*Egsyersteleen*,' he says, and wheels himself away while the two boys jump up and down, shouting and laughing. Dad throws out more coins to the two ragged boys as the lights change, then winds up the window to stop any more of the muddy rain splashing in. As he drives away he wipes the rain off his forearm, glances into the rear-view mirror to smile at me.

'Is it good to be home?' he asks.

'Yes,' I say.

I turn in my seat to watch the two boys. As they run off I see that the two bottom-cheeks of one of the boys are exposed out of holes in his shorts. There are more holes than material in his clothes. He and his street-urchin friend dance off, kicking water at each other from the puddles forming in the potholes in the road. They look happier than the people huddling under the bus shelter, many of them with plastic bags over their hair to keep it dry.

'What did the beggar say, Mum?' I ask.

'"*Egsyersteleen*". It means "May God give to you". The response to that is "*Abro esteleen*". It means "May God give to us all".'

'*Abro . . . ?*' Dad asks.

'*Abro esteleen.*'

'*Abro esteleen,*' Dad says.

'*Abro esteleen,*' I repeat from the back seat. Soon I'll start Amharic lessons with Yirdaw. Yirdaw was imprisoned and tortured during the Derg reign, his father was killed by Mengistu. Mum says Yirdaw is a very gentle man. Mum has already begun her lessons with him, and already speaks the beginnings of a simple, clear Amharic, and can read Ge'ez, the Amharic alphabet. She deciphers the signs on the side of the road for us as we drive along, one letter at a time. She has always learned the languages of the countries that have been our homes, speaking Kiswahili in Kenya, Urdu in Pakistan, and Sudanese Arabic, which is different from the Arabic she learned as a child in Haifa, which she has now mostly forgotten. She speaks languages simply and with no pretension, the way she does all things, with an uncluttered focus on one thing at a time, one word at a time. She would start as soon as we arrived in a new country, in the kitchen usually, or walking around the garden, pointing at things and asking for the translation.

'*Baba-Ji, yeh kya hai?* What is this?' she'd say, pointing at a loaf of bread, or a tea cosy in the kitchen. He would approach it with his milky, cataract-filmed eyes.

'*Yeh "tee cozee" hai,*' Baba-Ji would reply, and they would laugh together.

I turn back in my seat so that I am facing forward again; the street boys and the leper have disappeared from view behind us.

'Isn't leprosy contagious?' I ask.

'No, I don't think so,' Mum says. 'Leprosy isn't thought of in the same way any more. They all used to be up on the Jimma Road in a leper colony – remember, Allen?' she says. 'Some wonderful people used to look after them there, and they managed to make beautiful crafts even though they had no fingers. Amazing, really. Nobody else would touch them. Even now people don't want to touch them. But nowadays leprosy is treatable.'

We're reaching what feels like a crossroads at the heart of the city. We halt at traffic lights in a sea of blue and white *matatu* taxis, next to a giant statue of a majestic crowned lion, one paw resting on what looks like a giant boulder. My father points up the hill, at a wide avenue stretching away from us.

'It's not a good day for it, but if you look up the hill you'll see the train station. The French built the railway line which runs from here all the way to Djibouti on the Red Sea. That's north. Keep going in that direction' – he points ahead of us, west, to the Jimma Road – 'and eventually you'll end up on the border with Sudan, southern Sudan. If you head further north, through Tigray, and cross into northern Sudan you'll come to where we camped in the desert when we were in Khartoum. Do you remember camping by the pyramids at Meroué?'

'Does the railway line still work?' I ask. I like the sound of travelling across Ethiopia by train.

'Only really for cargo. You can travel on it, but it only comes in once or twice a week, and sometimes doesn't show up for days. Our Dutch friend who worked for Médecins Sans Frontières tried to travel to Djibouti on that train. He showed up at the station and sat on the platform for two days before it arrived.'

We all laugh.

'Your father and I used to go to a wonderful Italian restaurant up there by the station, in the old days. Do you remember, Allen?' Mother says. 'I wonder what happened to that family. They were an Italian family, they came here when Mussolini invaded Ethiopia and I don't think they ever left, not even during the troubles. Mind you, the old Italian families are Ethiopian now. They've intermarried with Ethiopians and they speak beautiful Italian and Amharic, it's wonderful to hear them switching between languages with such ease.'

We leave the city centre and head towards the outskirts, then turn off a tarmac road and onto a clay one. We slow down, navigate the muddy potholes which overflow as the tyres sink into them. We have our windows wide open now that the rain has stopped; I lean out of mine and let the evening air soak into me, with its smell of wood fires and smoke and rain and soil: the smell of home. We crawl uphill, the four-wheel drive bending and straining and the antenna swinging so widely it almost touches the false banana palms and bougainvillea bushes that crowd into the road.

'Nearly home now. We're just at the top over there.'

We round a bend and stop before a grey tin gate. The thin walls either side of the gate strain under a purple bougainvillea. Dad hoots once, a dog barks, and the gate is flung open by Tekelle the night watchman. The house is simple, two-storey, with a balcony that overlooks the garden. The garden is a mass of bougainvillea and palms and eucalyptus trees. A skinny dog dashes out from the side of the house. Tekelle shakes our hands warmly.

'Welcome,' he says. We are home.

Tsige, our cook, brings us strong Ethiopian coffee on a tray with tiny cups. The coffee is dense black, and thick. As Mum pours it out I choose a small fat banana from a branch of bananas in the fruit basket that looks as though it has just been cut from the tree in the garden. The bananas are all short and thick, so swollen they are almost round, bursting out of their thin skins, crowded together on the branch so I have to slip my fingers up to where the banana joins the branch and twist carefully. It is raining again, so we can't be outside in the garden and Anna, Mum and I have gathered in the living room. The inside of the house is full of dark wood. Dark wood floors, dark wood furniture that came with the house.

'And then what happened?' I ask.

Anna is lying on the sofa, propped up by cushions. She can't sit up properly because she has bruising all over her legs and back. Anna arrived in Ethiopia the week before I did. She has finished at boarding school now and came out before me to look for work in an orphanage. Mother is shaking her head, recalling the details of the story. Anna and Mum were attacked in an asylum.

'We thought we were walking into the orphanage,' Anna says, 'but it turns out one side of the building is actually an insane asylum. We could hear this man shouting, and I could tell that the noise was coming closer. You know that feeling you get when you just know you're about to be singled out?' I nod. 'Well, we turned around to look and there was this huge, crazy man with a big stick, and when he saw us he came running at us with his stick.' Anna waves her arms in the air brandishing an imaginary stick. 'Everyone scattered. I told Mum to run and we both ran in different directions but he followed me and hit me across the back with his stick and knocked me to the ground, then he just kept whacking me.'

I put my hand over my mouth, Anna shakes her head. I think we might both be about to laugh.

'It was terrifying,' Mum says. 'I could hear Anna screaming and I saw her on the ground being beaten, and there was nothing I could do. Thankfully a group of men appeared and managed to overpower him momentarily, and Anna and I ran and hid in a tin hut with Yeshi, Anna's friend.'

'It looked like a storage hut for grain,' Anna says. 'He was bashing at the door and the roof with his stick and all these dents were appearing in it. Like in the films.' We laugh at this idea.

'Then what happened?'

'Then more men came running and they got him to the ground and tied him up.'

'What with?'

'Just with ropes,' Anna says. 'They carried him away, still shouting, all tied up with ropes, like an animal.' She shakes her head, looking sorry.

'Poor man,' Mum agrees. 'Poor Anna. It was really terrifying.'

Mum hands me banana bread on a plate and I hold it on my lap, waiting. I want to hear all the remaining details of the story first. Mum and Anna tell stories well.

'And Yeshi was so sweet, wasn't she, Mum? She was so apologetic, as if it was her fault. She works in the orphanage but she has actually been in the asylum herself, as a patient. There's something not right about her, but she helps the Sisters look after the children.' Anna taps the side of her head in imitation of Yeshi. 'She kept saying, "Me no cracked, me Sister."' We all laugh.

'So poor Anna has been lying on this sofa all week and has hardly seen anything of Addis,' Mother says. I wonder if Anna minds that.

'Does it still hurt?' I ask.

'I'm OK now. I couldn't walk very well for a day or two. Then yesterday Mum and I went for a short walk just out the gate and around the neighbourhood and we were chased by kids shouting "*Ferangi! Ferangi!*" It wasn't exactly relaxing. Did you hear the kids shouting it at you on your way from the airport?'

I nod. I did hear. It means 'foreigner'. I'm sure it won't take us long to feel at home, though. We just need to find some bit of Ethiopia that feels like ours.

'White people are only just starting to come back, now that Mengistu has gone, so they're not used to seeing white faces,' Mum says. 'That's all it is.'

'And it's poured with rain all week.' Anna adds.

'It's the long rains, unfortunately. I wish your first visit could have been in the dry season, but it will be hot down in the Rift Valley. And it's sometimes sunny in the morning then builds to a storm in the afternoon, so mornings are best for getting out and exploring. You're not seeing Addis at its best, but you will.' Mum reaches out and holds Anna's leg, then pulls the blanket down so her feet are covered.

I pull a shawl around my shoulders. I slept with it wrapped around me on the plane, but I didn't think I'd need it here. Addis is much colder than I thought it would be. We are high here, over seven thousand feet.

'More banana bread, anyone?' Mum asks.

'No thanks, Mum. That was just like Siddiq's banana bread.' The highest compliment we can give a banana bread is that it resembles our Pakistani cook's. Siddiq came to us from the Italian Embassy, and though he couldn't speak English he could sing in Italian, and loved to sing his Pakistani version of Italian opera in the kitchen in a strange high-pitched voice, mixing Urdu and Italian words, slapping at flies with the teacloth, wiping at his sweating forehead as he worked.

'Mum, can't you get Siddiq to stop singing?' we'd ask. 'It's really annoying.'

'No, I can't,' she'd say. 'It would hurt his feelings.'

I wonder what Siddiq is doing now. Pakistan seems like another lifetime already. We are back in Africa, where we belong.

We look out at the wet beyond the windows. A low mist hangs over a suddenly darkening and breathless garden. Tsige comes in from the kitchen with a tray to clear away the cups.

'Poor Anna,' she says. She shakes her head. 'This man, he was crazy. He very bad man, *bataam metfo*, very bad man.' Then Tsige smiles and we all laugh again.

'I'll give you a lift home, Tsige,' Mum says, 'it's still so wet out there.'

'Thank you, Madam.' Tsige leaves to change into her home clothes. I know we are going to like Tsige. She is strong and calm. She has a small scar in the shape of a cross on her forehead. I've already seen a few of those. I'll ask her about it tomorrow, and ask her to start teaching me Amharic.

When Mum and Tsige have left, Anna and I sit on the sofa together. 'It's not really what I expected,' Anna confides. 'It's nothing like Kenya.'

I agree. And it's nothing like the pictures in the photograph albums. In the last weak light from the garden the Ethiopian crosses on the wall shine gently. They have come home after all these years in foreign countries.

'Dad says Langano is much more like the Africa we know,' Anna says. 'It's one of the lakes in the Rift Valley. It's hot. And we can swim in the lake.'

'When are we going?' I ask.

'I think this Friday. Day after tomorrow,' Anna says. She rubs at her lower back, grimaces. 'I can't wait.'

'Me too,' I say.

I leave Anna and open my suitcase on the floor of my new bedroom. There's not much in the room: a plain single bed, a swept floor, a cupboard, a desk. On the bedside table are some wild flowers my mother or Abeji, the gardener, has picked from the garden. They sprout unevenly from a small Nigerian jug. Mum always places flowers from the garden by our beds when we come home. I look at them. I feel the ease of being here, of being home, sinking into me. I think of Mum driving down the hill with Tsige in the passenger seat; Mum's fine gold bangles, four of them, will be swaying on her right wrist, on her bare brown arm. Her cousin June gave them to her in Lebanon. Mum went to Lebanon for a year to learn Arabic and French after she finished at her Catholic convent school in England. She learned French, which she speaks clearly and fluently, but she didn't learn as much Arabic, though she wishes she had. She spoke Arabic as a child in Haifa.

Mum's bangles will be clinking together as they bump over potholes, and the neighbourhood kids will be running after them, shouting. It doesn't occur to me to ask Mum if she minds the kids shouting '*Ferangi*', because I know she doesn't.

An ant is picking its way over the slender prickles of the bougainvillea stem in the vase by my bed. I hold out my finger and rest it on the stem, in the ant's path. I wait for it to crawl onto my fingertip so that I can examine it up close. When I get back to boarding school I'll be applying for British universities; I'll apply for Oxford to study biology. If I get the place I'll take a gap year, a year off, and travel. I'd like to travel in Ethiopia first, to get to know this country that I am impatient to recognise as my home – after all, I was born here. That must mean something. And Ethiopia has been so much of our family story that I feel I already know it, that I have a learned affection for the country from our parents. I wonder whether there are Kenya-style *siafu* here, safari ants with giant heads and pincers, or the clumsy flying termites with fat bodies and weak wings, which taste of peanut butter. After the rains we would catch them as they streamed in towards the strip light in the kitchen. We'd hand them to our ayah Deborah, who would pull off their wings and fry them quickly to a dark brown.

I stand by the window and look into the dark garden. I push the window open. The rain has stopped again. I can't see enough to make out the shape of the garden, the plants we have here, but I can smell the eucalyptus trees and the heavy, rain-filled, smoke-scented air; and there is something else I can smell, something that smells different from Kenya's smell. It's an old, musky sort of smell, a Three Wise Men amber and myrrh and frankincense smell; that, mixed with eucalyptus – that's what this smell is. I breathe it in deeply.

I hear Tekelle calling out to someone on the other side of the gate. I'm impatient to go out and explore, to swim in the lake and start rooting down in this new country. Then a few more terms at school and I'll be able to come back here, at the beginning of my gap year, before I go to university in England.

Maybe, once I'm at university, England will start feeling a bit more like home too, and the odd thing will have been ironed out by then. I think of Matron, and the cleaners Mary and Jean, with their suspicions. I have a bad feeling about what I've been doing at school, especially now that I am here. I know it's wrong. I'd be so ashamed if anyone found out. I'll get rid of that habit soon enough. But I don't need to think about that, not while I'm here and life has returned to normal.

I turn from the window and start unpacking my suitcase, flattening my clothes with the palm of my hand against the bed to ease out the creases, then hanging them up, neatly, sparsely, in the cupboard as I practise the new words I have learned. *Maquina*, car. *Goma*, tyre. *Bataam metfo*, very bad. *Abro esteleen*, May God give to us all.

Dad in the bush with his Piper. Kenya.

PART III:
OXFORD
1994-1998

My first school, Maseru Prep. Lesotho, 1979.

Ten

Oxford University. March 1995.
Twenty years old

In the dream, I know that I must finish the binge. If I can just finish it then I can join in, I can pay attention to the other situation that makes the sides of my jaw ache with anxiety, that makes my teeth ache when I wake up in my room on the ground floor, St John's quad. It's a regularly occurring dream, once things get bad. Which they do, quickly unravelling, once I arrive at Oxford, and overtaking the moderate habit I'd begun at boarding school, turning it into something else altogether.

I was looking forward to starting at university. I was harder and leaner, or so I thought. I thought my year of travelling had changed me. I'd applied for a deferred place at Oxford and had returned to Ethiopia to work for a few months at the start of my gap year, then I had travelled with a boyfriend on the Asian subcontinent for several months, with no more than a small backpack and a sleeping bag, proud of the little we had to carry.

On a bright Kerala morning in south India, I saw myself in a mirror for the first time after many months. I had gone alone to a simple low building standing on its own at the far end of a field, its corrugated tin roof tilting down to where a family of pigs played in the dust, and in a bright polished mirror looked back at my face, at my long sun-bleached hair, and saw that I had changed. I was several months older, and I was thin.

Perhaps I had been thin for many months, but I had not noticed. I had not seen more than a small browned square of mirror, customarily tacked to the wall of the lodgings usually near the poorly lit showers, and above a concrete sink with its block of blue soap for hand-washing. But here in the shined mirror, in the full sun of mid-morning, I saw that the heaviness of my face had melted away, my eyes were bigger and greener, my shoulders were lean and defined. The black-haired woman from the waxing place, a Kerala woman, dark-skinned, smiled back at me in the mirror as she stirred the hot wax. She pointed at my eyebrows in the mirror, ran her finger over one of her own eyebrows.

'Threading?' she asked.

'No, thank you,' I said. I shook my head, still watching my unfamiliar face. I like my eyebrows thick, like this.

I looked at my lips, at my collarbone, at the long, defined biceps of my arms. For all the months we had been in India, travelling slowly from the north to the south, we had eaten sparingly, from street stalls mainly, saving our dollars for the long journey we planned to make across Southeast Asia. We were sometimes hungry, but mostly it was part of the thrill and the challenge of the journey, doing it that way, with nothing spare, nothing wasted.

I watched her arms, the ring on her second toe, the red *choli* shifting against her midriff as she crouched over the wax, lifting it on a wooden spoon and letting it spill back, golden, glistening, to check its consistency. There was no difference between us, in the slightness of our bodies.

'Come,' she said. She patted the bed she wanted me to lie on so she could reach the hairs on my legs. I stood and unwrapped my *kikoy*. I lay down on the bed. I was graceful, I was like her, I didn't take up any more space than I needed to.

I was happy to be changed; change was what was meant to happen when you went away for a year, like this. I lay still in the hut with its slanting roof and listened to the sounds of the pigs and the chickens outside. I felt a soft thrill under my skin.

But now that I am here and the terms are slipping through my fingers I know that I am doing it all wrong. It didn't take long for it to spin away from me. And just like in the dream that keeps coming back, the reality is that I know that if I can just finish the binge, if I can just finish it off, I can come back and join in again.

In the dream there is an endless, never-ending table of food, and I scour it, choosing the foods for my plate. Others mill around me, choosing theirs, on sensible, restrained plates. At a table somewhere in the large garden is a group of my friends, who are eating normally. They haven't noticed yet what I'm doing. I see my sister. She is talking to someone, laughing, holding her buffet plate. She chooses a chocolate square, then wanders away.

In front of me are soulless piles of chocolate tiffin squares. There are prawns sticking out of red sauces in giant silver-coloured dinner-lady tubs, there are deep-fried Chinese-style fritters, there are gaudy puddings in bright colours, pyramids of sticky-shiny gulab jamun. I pile my plate and pile my plate but I can't get back to my table to eat. When I look down I realise I don't have enough. I go back to the buffet tables, I carry on.

I have to finish the binge because I know they are getting closer. There has been a murder. I did it. In the cavernous house, with so many rooms I am lost within it, there's a bedroom that contains my suitcase. It is open, spilling clothes across the otherwise empty room. I must finish packing. But first I have to finish this binge.

I'm in the room now, but the more I try to pack, the more the chaos spreads. There are piles of clothes and possessions everywhere, spilling from an open cupboard, strewn across the floor and the bathroom. I've left it too late to sort it out. It won't all fit in my suitcase. I look around the room, in the cavernous house. I can't possibly pack in time. It's hopeless. I must get back to the tables of food, at once.

If I can just finish the binge, I'll be free. But I never have the pleasure of eating the food in my dream, of biting into the chocolate tiffins in aching, anxious piles. Instead, I wake with my mouth empty, with my teeth hurting, and my jaw clenched and tight. It's just a dream. Thank God I am not there, with the crowds of people and the buffet tables, with the perpetual choice of food I can't eat and in the grip of a chain of events I can't stop. I'm not there, I'm here. I'm here in my room in Oxford.

I keep my eyes closed. I can't yet open them to the day, to the light pushing in around the sides of the curtains in my room. I lie still, hearing voices and footsteps crossing the college's main quadrangle. My room is at the heart of the college, its old stained-glass window unblinking onto the square. As you enter through the porters' lodge there it is on the corner leading to St Johns' quad. On the opposite side is the chapel and, beyond that, the Cloisters. Opposite the porters' lodge is the President's house. Magdalen is not as grand, or as austere, as some colleges. It is softened by the deer and the loop of wayward river, and the tower that swims up to the sky.

Nobody seemed to know about the room that I find myself inhabiting. It was somehow overlooked in the rooms ballot, so even though I came low down on the ballot, it was still free and I quickly chose it, with its stained glass and ancient carved stonework. The only drawback is the distance to the bathroom and the toilet; perhaps that's why nobody wanted to live here. A cold stone staircase leads to the bathroom two floors above. I didn't think this would be a problem for me, but I hadn't really thought it through, hadn't wanted to think about how often I need the privacy of the bathroom.

It is still my secret. Nobody knows about it. It happens all the time now, almost every day at the moment, and sometimes more than that, on really bad days. It's been a bad term, this one. Hilary term. It comes after Michaelmas, I've learned, and before Trinity. I'll wipe it out, Hilary term. Trinity will be different.

I touch my stomach. I run my tongue over the ridges on the inside of my cheeks. My bladder is full, which is not a good sign. I'm so thirsty when it's all over that I drink and drink; I can't drink enough to quench my thirst. In the night I have to climb the stone steps to the bathroom, up and down, up and down. Patches of rose light play across the darkness behind my lids and I think back, slowly, tentatively, to the night before, wanting to prolong the floating dark before I have to face what I know I did.

I climb the steps, each one worn at its middle. I close the large wooden door, run the bath, take off my clothes and lay them on the chair. I line up the shampoo and soap on the side of the bath, the toothbrush and toothpaste on the side of the sink. I would prefer to have a shower to start again with, but there is no shower, just a bath with two taps. I have a plastic jug I use to mix the hot and cold water to rinse off my hair after I've washed it, but I know there is a better method.

My scout, who cleans my room three times a week, tells me I should buy a rubber hose attachment with two arms that fit over the taps, combining the hot and the cold and ending in a shower head. I ask her where I can buy one. She says Anywhere. I ask Where More Specifically and she says Woolworths. I think I have seen a Woolworths on Cornmarket. I must get to Woolworths. But first I have to write my genetics essay, I have to take my reading list to the library, I have to find my lost copy of *The Selfish Gene*. I have to take control of my eating. I have exams looming at the end of term. There are so many more urgent things I have to do first, so for now the jug will have to do.

I float in the water of the bath, my hair fans around me. My ears are under the water, muffling out sound. I'm in a hiatus, the pause after the storm. I haven't yet begun my day, not really, with its constant battles against the urge that keeps pricking at me like a bully I can't shake off. I can't lose it again today. I can't keep going like this. There are just so many other things I could be focusing on, things I want to focus on, things I want to do. And I have a university squash match at five, so whatever happens it will have to wait until after that is over. I pull the plug, climb out of the bath, dress.

In my room I open the curtains. I sit in a pool of sunshine and cover my eyelashes in black mascara. It's fine now for the light to come in, for passers-by to glance towards the room in the corner of the quadrangle whose windows reflect the light at odd angles, it's fine because I am up now, and this can be a day like anybody else's day.

I make the bed, stretching the fitted sheet tightly across it and tucking it firmly under the mattress. I want no wrinkles in the sheet, no specks of dust, no crumbs. I clear away the clothes into the wardrobe. I tidy the desk, arrange papers in one neat pile at one end, collect pens and pencils in a pot. Then I clear the room. I take the *kikoy* off the low table, carry it outside and shake it over the grass, replace it straightened and flat, its stripes aligned with the sides of the table. I empty the ashtray. I place the succulent in its plant pot in the middle of the table. On the floor between the low table and the wood-panelled wall I have laid a foam mattress which I cover with an embroidered bedspread from a shop on the hill that leads to the old train station in Addis, and I arrange cushions along it, against the wall.

I gather food wrappers and crumbs, ends of bread and empty food containers in a plastic bag which I tie at the top and leave by the door to take to the bin outside. I don't want the scout to see the incriminating quantity of food debris in my waste-paper basket. I carry mugs and plates and a small bottle of washing-up liquid up the stone staircase back to the bathroom, where I fill the sink with water and scrub out the mugs and plates, then polish them dry till they shine, till there is no sign. I carry it all downstairs, collect my kettle and return to the bathroom. I rinse out the flakes of limescale, wipe the greasy fingerprints off the kettle, and fill it with clean gushing water.

Everything is in order. The room is as I want it to be, welcoming and bright and blameless, the curtains pushed as wide open as they can go. A version of ordinary life happens here too: friends pass through here often, we have parties, stay up late, drink coffee and roll cigarettes between lectures and essays and exams. People like coming to my room. They lie on my covered day bed or sit at the chair at my desk, and I make them coffee and we laugh about normal things. When I don't want them to come in I just lock the door and pretend I am not here.

The room as it is now – warm, open, nothing to hide – is the room my friends see, and the boyfriend who visits me from his university further north, the same boyfriend I travelled with on my gap year. He comes to see me at weekends and I often go to see him too. We have easy, typical weekends, sleeping late, going to pubs, walking through Christchurch meadows. He doesn't think much of Oxford, is my impression; he thinks my friends here are square and uptight; sometimes I agree with him. He has no idea about the other side of me; none of them do.

I flick on the kettle. I sit at my desk with two blank pieces of paper. 'TODAY,' I write at the top of one, and I fill out my movements hour by hour, my goals for the day.

10am: Zoology Library
11am: Lecture
12pm: Library – start essay
1pm: Lunch, in Hall
2pm–4pm: Essay

4pm: Back to college, get ready for squash match
5pm: Meet at van outside Queen's
6pm: Squash match
7pm: Eat at squash club.

Every hour must be accounted for. I examine the list. I don't
want to set myself something I can't achieve. I don't know if I
am a good judge of what is realistic for me. And I know that just
one small failure in the day can derail the whole thing.

I have the same dichotomous thinking with food; I have
become fearful of the foods I usually eat in a binge. Some foods
I can't touch, outside of the binge, because I fear it will trigger
another binge. Cream cakes, chocolates, biscuits, sausage rolls,
even just a taste of them can bring it crashing in on itself. It's
better if I just avoid them altogether.

At the top of the other sheet of paper I write 'HEALTHY
FOOD' and underline it. I list foods I can keep in my small
whirring fridge and on the shelf above it: healthy, unthreatening,
non-binge-triggering foods. Cereals and Cheddar cheese,
bananas and pesto sauce and pita bread.

Birdsong fills the room from the lawns outside. Peace. The
peace is precious, I feel myself floating on it. I hardly dare
breathe for fear of shattering it, this simple peace that takes me
back to another time, to the chicken we kept in our rabbit run
when I was five years old. I remember his rust-gold feathers and
strong, sinewed chicken feet as he pecked at the grain I fed
him.

At my desk, I close my eyes so that light falls onto my face
from the window, and the warm, still feeling comes back to me
as I remember the chicken. I want to replace the unease I feel

after the dream. I know that I have lost this still feeling here at Oxford, and I know that I need to get it back. I sit without moving, on the child's chair I bring out from my bedroom, watching the chicken, watching the firefinches out of the corner of my eye pecking in the dust around the drain cover. The African firefinch and the delicate red-cheeked cordon-bleu with red patches on its cheeks. Mum teaches us the names of the birds. When I have finished watching the chicken I leave the firefinch and go down to find my brother and sister in the creek, *swish, swish, swish,* using a long blade of grass as a *panga*, swinging at the tall grass on either side of me.

I check the time. I need to get to Zoology for 10 a.m. I gather up my books, reluctant to leave the reinstated calm of my room. I am back to normal now. There is a knock at my window. It's a friend from the course. I leap up and run out to join him. We walk arm in arm through the porters' lodge and up Hollywell Street to our lecture. I know I can have a good day today, I will have a good day today. There is no reason why I shouldn't.

Eleven

Oxford University. May 1995

Dr Roberts touches his fingertips together in front of his beard and observes me kindly. 'I have no doubt, Caroline, that you will pass your Prelims,' he says. 'We all have the utmost confidence in you. That is why we offered you the place at Magdalen.'

He crosses to the other side of the room and fiddles with the bolt of the centuries-old window frames, then with both hands forces the lower half upwards. It's a beautiful, still, spring day and the cool air that flows into the room smells of an earthy leafiness. He stays for a moment looking out.

We are on the first floor of New Building with its four floors of high-ceilinged rooms and tall eighteenth-century windows that face onto green lawns stretching to the Cloisters. The Cloisters are carved out of a cold stone and hung with mossed gargoyles over the parapets. In the wrong frame of mind, the Cloisters are dark and dank. The stone floors alongside the arches are worn to a dip in the middle from several hundred years of footsteps. But this wing of the college, New Building, is open, light, scarcely more than a couple of hundred years old. This stretch, a long classical building, stands on its own over here, distinct, separate; a mistake in architectural style, as though it was part of a forgotten bigger plan. Between us and the Cloisters, beyond a delicate wrought iron gate, is the deer park and an errant loop of river.

Dr Roberts stays a moment longer at the window, caught, as I am, by the stillness and promise of the day. Then he turns his back to the birdsong that drifts in from the deer park, and leans against the windowsill.

'Is it Prelims you are worried about?' he persists. 'Because really, there's nothing for you to worry about. Nothing at all.' He touches the pen in his shirt pocket, then slides it out, absently, and holds it between his fingers. 'In our tutorial yesterday you showed a very strong understanding of the principles of genetics; there is no doubt in my mind that you are capable of passing the exams and continuing to do very well in this course.' He slides his pen back into his pocket.

I don't share Dr Roberts' confidence. How I have managed to stay afloat so far through the essays and tutorials is a mystery to me. The two other students at my college on the same course seem to take it all in effortlessly, almost as if they knew it all already. But each new essay topic, each new subject I feel I grapple with bodily. At every step forward I seem to become more conscious of the bareness of my knowledge, aware that every fact I take on is a mercurial entity, is just the tip of a mass of further academia and learning that feels beyond my reach. I have always been confident academically, but something has changed.

At some level I must understand the overall concepts: that must be what redeems me in Dr Roberts' eyes. It's true, I can retain the poetic or the satisfyingly logical. I know that genotype is the genetic makeup, while phenotype is the behavioural and physical expression of that genetic makeup. The layer underlying and the surface layer. And I can recite the meiotic phases because if you repeat them enough they begin to sound poetic, flowing fluidly one from the other like the Latin declensions I learned at prep school in Kenya. But when it comes to the mass of detail, I'm deluged; it feels beyond my grasp.

On a flipchart behind Dr Roberts' head are his drawings from yesterday's tutorial. Arrows branch from one set of chromosomes to another. 'Homologous recombination', 'diploid', 'haploid', 'spindle fibres': his words are scratched over the page, connecting with arching arrows to points on the meiotic process. On some level it makes sense to me, though I can't be certain even of that, that it will not slip away from me. Mostly it seeps into a more general feeling of drowning, of not quite being in control in any way, which I have felt since I arrived at Oxford at the beginning of the academic year. Friendships, timetables, lectures, essay deadlines, the frantic eight-week terms with Latin names: I don't have a grip on any of it most of the time. Even finding my way around town is a challenge. I carry a map with me everywhere I go, and twice already I've had to spread it over my desk in my room and tape together its thinning folds.

The only things with reliable, predictable surfaces and edges, with ease and the promise of completion, are the different foods I've discovered around the city. In the corner shop next to the King's Arms, in the supermarkets on Cornmarket and down the Cowley Road, and in the shop in the covered market opposite the butcher, where skinned and sinewed game hangs in rows from hooks. And then there are the dinner ladies in college Hall, who serve up generous and plentiful beef and Yorkshire puddings, chicken pie, fish in batter, pork chops, potatoes, gravy, lamb stews and solid sponge puddings with as much hot, thick custard as I can cradle in one bowl. And there's the woman in the college tuck shop, when everything else is shut.

My staple is the supermarkets for the reliable cheap fodder of binges, the two-for-one Maryland cookies, own-brand custard creams, and orange Club biscuits on discount, the pints of milk, loaves of bread, packs of butter, cream cakes on the expiry date – none of it need last till the next day. I buy it cheap and in plenty so I know I will not run out of food before the end of the binge, and find myself falling calamitously off some ledge.

Ink from the pen in Dr Roberts' pocket has spread a small circle of blue on his shirt. He's sitting down now, on his comfortable chair, absent-mindedly running his fingers over a fraying patch on the armrest. It's that kind of day, the kind that draws you out towards the window and the sounds coming from the deer park.

I explain that while I am worried about the forthcoming exams, the real problem is that I don't think the course is right for me. I think I should be studying languages. He nods, but looks disappointed. He will inform the college of my decision and talk to the Modern Languages tutors.

My plan is set: I'll prepare for the interview with the languages tutors and if they accept me on their course I'll leave Oxford for the rest of the term, go somewhere where I can work on my languages and straighten myself out; then the following term, the start of the second academic year, after the summer at home in Ethiopia, I'll start again with a new course, one that I'm good at this time – I know I'm good at languages – and a new room, and I'll find the resolve, I'll find the strength and self-discipline, I'll find the clarity and some buried instinct of self-preservation, and the sense, the simple bloody sense, to change things.

Twelve

Summer holiday from Oxford.
Ethiopia. July 1995

My sister and I have been coming to Ethiopia for three years now, since our parents moved here when we were at boarding school. Anna and I come out at every opportunity from our universities in England, and William lives and works in Ethiopia now, on a conservation project in Awash National Park. He has graduated from his university in England with a degree in environmental sciences and has come back to live in Africa.

We have travelled with our parents all over the country, to Gondar and Aksum in the northern highlands, and over into Eritrea to the seaside port of Massawa, past the shells of tanks on the road from Eritrea's sporadic war with Ethiopia. We've camped in the desert and in the far south in the Omo, on the border with Kenya. But every time we are here we come back to Lake Langano, a bumpy two-hundred-kilometre, three-hour drive south into the Rift Valley: leave Addis, turn right at the junction at Mojo, then one hundred kilometres of red road;

then, as the road dwindles to a dirt trail running alongside the shores of Langano, stop to engage the differential lock, and a steep, uneven climb down to the hut by the lake.

I love the bareness and emptiness of the brown lake, with the hot, hot sun burning into all of it: the brown water, the corrugated tin roof of the hut, my back when I swim. Getting down to the lake without flip-flops is treacherous, even after Usi has swept the path, because thorns drop from the acacia, a flat-topped East African acacia with a dusted yellow bark. It stretches over the left of the path just a few metres from the hut's thatched veranda. We had a fire under the tree last night, and barbecued our meat, tendered by its marinade and the journey in the cold box down here from Addis. The marinade is a recipe from our Pakistani cook Siddiq, and Tsige copied it out into a lined exercise book in the kitchen. There is no fridge here at the lake, no electricity, no running water. The kitchen is just a small outhouse with shelves for the powdered milk and the jam, a gas canister, and a cement sink for washing our dishes in water Usi brings up in buckets from the lake.

The pigeons scratch and coo on the roof. The same sounds woke me yesterday, will wake us every day we spend at the lake, sounds that merge with the heat, become the heat, then separate, lift out, lifting me out of deep sun-baked sleep.

I walk down the path shading my eyes against the morning sun. At the lake I take off my *kikoy*, lay it on the sand, kick off my flip-flops, wade into the water. The water is brown, clean. I dive in and swim. Four of breast stroke, four strokes of crawl, four of butterfly, then I dive under, eyes open, flying through the water, surrounded, held, no sound. Up for breath then under again, swimming out.

Nobody knows how deep this lake is. Two days ago when we arrived from Addis my brother, sister and I swam out and dared each other to dive down as far as we could go, swimming through light-filtered brownness, down, down, down, knowing there is no bottom, coming up euphoric and shouting out and gasping for air, swimming over an abyss in this volcanic lake in a deep Rift Valley crack in the earth.

I'm awake and alive. *Stroke, stroke, stroke*, as the muscles under my armpits, along the sides of my ribs, stretch and pull and extend. Pulling out and further out. I turn back, morning light flickering off the lake. I'm not far out enough, I'll swim further so I can see it all, the emptiness, all the panorama of hut and escarpment and cattle trails in the dust. Then I turn again to look back at the shore. Dad is shaving in the lake, thigh-deep by the broken jetty inhabited by black cormorants. The sandy crescent of beach runs to a path that snakes up past the acacia to the foot of the steps. And rising up beyond the hut the red, hot escarpment. I can see the cattle trails that wind down from its crest, down its barren dust-slopes where only thorny scrub grows. When we are out on the lake in the rubber dinghy with its outboard motor, exploring the far shore – a wilderness of giant fig trees and colobus and colonies of pelicans – Dad has taught us to look for the cattle trails, which guide us back to our hut on the western shore.

I tread water. Tomorrow I'd like to wake earlier, to see this at dawn. From this distance the hut is one splash of red bougain-villea, a glint of sunbeams off the tin roof. Dad rinses his razor in the lake, holds a mirror close to his strong chin, head back, mouth to the side, reaching the hair in the awkward place. He shakes the razor and small droplets of water fall back into the lake. I think of the hippos in the Mara River, snorting behind

Dad as he shaved. There is a hippo in this lake too. Perhaps it's
under me now, somewhere down there in the depths.

My brother is on the shore now. We wave to each other. The
wildlife conservation project that William is working on is a few
hundred kilometres from here, in the east of the country. Their
voices come out to me over the water. William's hair is long, in
blond curls. His body is strong and brown. He wears an anklet
and a leather necklace. His arms are folded under his nipples.
He and Dad talk as Dad continues to shave. Then William
wades in, dives, swims a powerful butterfly whose ripples run
back and splash against my father's legs.

I wonder if I am brave enough to swim down on my own. I
look at my hand under the water. A foot under the water and
I can no longer see it. Hippos like the shallows. Like bilharzia
snails they tend to live around the margins of the lake. There is
no bilharzia in this lake.

I dive under, swim straight down, strong strokes; the light
refracts to a dark brownness. I wonder what creatures live down
here. One more stroke and my ears start to ache, my lungs stretch.
It's getting darker, I might not know which way is back up. I turn
back on myself and swim as fast as I can back towards the light –
one, two, start letting the breath out now, one more stroke, one
more stroke and I'm there, I'm out, gulping air, elated.

I turn on my back, float as I watch the sky. Oxford is so far
away that it's hard to believe it really exists, my college with its
exaggerated tower, its chameleon green grass, the dinner ladies
in Hall, and the constant struggle since I arrived there to keep
up, to keep my head above water. Time moves so quickly there
and I don't feel I have a handle on things. It's already the end
of the first year.

Madrid feels far away too. I lived there for a few months after I left my course, to get my Spanish ready for next term. My French is fine; I speak it instinctively because I have been learning it all my life, but my Spanish is much weaker. By the end of my Madrid stay my Spanish was beginning to spill out easily, fluidly. It helped having Spanish boyfriends. I'm no longer with my old boyfriend who I travelled with on my gap year – we have gone our separate ways. Perhaps it is a good thing, a clean start for my second year, staying in one place, not shifting constantly back and forth between his university and mine, always feeling like I want to be somewhere else.

I know for certain now that I am not well, that what began as a habit at boarding school has transformed into something else entirely. I have to stop it, but perhaps it is only a matter of effort and of time. I still have time. I have two more academic years there, after this one. If I just applied myself to it, focused on it, I know I could overcome it. I just need to try harder, and I need to work harder too. I've brought my textbooks with me so I can do the required reading for my course. The bag of books is against the wall of the hut, underneath my camp bed. I'll bring it out later.

The cattle are coming down, their humps flapping above the dust. Darsa, Anna's favourite of the herding kids, drives them with a stick; his head looks bigger than his body, his tummy bulges, he can't be more than six years old. He is naked but for shorts, and runs barefoot alongside the cattle. Behind him is his older sister, who carries the baby in a sling; she picks her way more carefully. Darsa and his sisters have just one tuft of hair at the front of the head and the rest of it is shaved clean. Tsige told us that this is so that they can be pulled up to heaven by this tuft when the time comes. It makes it easier to pull them up if there's something to grip.

Anna is there too, under a tree by the shore, lying on a *kikoy*, reading. But now she sits up, distracted by the cattle, and calls out to Darsa and his sister. They wave back to her. She watches the cattle, watches Darsa's sister with the baby. The cattle bend their heads to the lake, thin-legged, jostling. Darsa puts down his stick and walks to the water's edge. He looks back to Anna to make sure she is watching before he jumps into the lake, naked. He launches himself into a front crawl she has been trying to teach him and his siblings. Sharp little elbows and legs protrude from the lake; he swims as long as he can, then bursts out of the water to breathe, panting and trying to be bold. He hasn't learned yet how to breathe between strokes. After Anna showed them the basics of swimming yesterday she pulled them around on the old surfboard Dad keeps in a shed and they screamed with terror and delight. She said they wriggled like slippery fish.

Mum is on the shore now, a *kikoy* around her waist; Dad is next to her, wet. He swam after his shave. He embraces her and she pushes him away, laughing. She waves to us, both arms above her head the way Dad has told us to do if we get into trouble out at sea.

'Breakfast,' she calls across the water.

William and I race each other back towards the shore. Breakfast will be last night's potatoes fried over the gas ring connected to the gas canister. Potatoes fried with onions which we'll eat with fried eggs and tomatoes, with bread Tsige baked in Addis. The butter is in the cold box, with icepacks and a lingering smell of marinated meat. On the third night, once our icepacks have melted and our provisions have gone, we'll drive the few kilometres along a dirt track at the top to the Wabe Shebelle, the almost empty lakeside hotel my parents used to visit when they were first in Ethiopia. There we'll eat *tebs*, strips of beef fried in spicy *berbere*.

After breakfast we sit on cushions on cane chairs in the shade of the veranda and read as we wait for the sun to arc towards the western shore. I go to the kitchen and pour boiled water from a jerrycan into the tin kettle. I light the gas flame and wait for the kettle to boil. Mum slices Tsige's banana bread and carries it out to the veranda, where Dad is tuning the short-wave radio to the BBC's *Focus on Africa*. We want to know what's happening in South Africa, down there at the bottom of our continent, now just into the second year of Mandela's rule, one year after the end of apartheid. Last night, as moths immolated themselves against the gas lamp hanging from the thatch, we listened again to Mandela's first Freedom Day speech, broadcast on the World Service.

Usi and Darsa have never heard of South Africa. Even Tsige, in the city, has not heard of it. She knows about Somalis, though – they are belligerent people. She doesn't like them. Nor does Marta, the housegirl from next door.

'They are black,' she said to my mother, shaking her head ominously, when a Somali family moved into a house down the bumpy road from us in Addis.

'But Marta,' Mum said, confused, 'aren't you black?'

'No, Madam,' she laughed. 'I am yellow.'

Usi is on his way up the path, carrying a bucket of lake water; he holds one arm out to balance himself. On the other side of the thornbrush boundary a naked Darsa and the cattle are on their way home. Their dust hangs in the heat over the escarpment long after they have disappeared.

Thirteen

Oxford University.
October 1995

Some way through the first term of my second year, finding myself mired again, I write a letter to my parents on blue airmail paper. I take one out of the pack in my drawer, open it up on my desk, smooth the thin paper out with my hands. I tie the hair out of my face so that I can think clearly, about how to present what I want to say so that it doesn't sound too discouraging. I write that I struggle sometimes with low mood and would like professional help. I don't mention my eating disorder; it is still my secret. 'Low mood' is a much easier way of phrasing it. My friend from college, Hugh, has found the name of a therapist, a psychoanalyst, he said, so I have someone I can approach. I tell my parents what the sessions would cost.

Then, to give a broader picture of things, to take things away from the heart of the matter, I write that I'm doing well. I describe a party I went to, and a walk in the deer park. I tell them about the kingfisher you can see on the river here, and I describe my new room in the corner of the eighteenth-century stretch of New Building.

Two weeks later I have my first meeting with Dr Brinke, the psychoanalyst. I'm perched awkwardly in his study, waiting for him to begin the session, but he says nothing. I feel I need to break the silence but I'm at a loss for what to say. After an uncomfortable minute he shifts slightly in his chair behind his large desk and asks me why I have come to see him.

'Oh, I'm not sure. Not exactly,' I say. I wish I had thought of an answer to this before I came here today. The truth is that I'm not sure exactly what is wrong. But if I don't know what the problem is, then how can Dr Brinke cure me? I must try to articulate, at the very least.

'I'm not very well,' I begin. This feels like a weak start. 'I don't know what the problem is. I don't know if I'm just depressed or if there's something else wrong with me. I also . . .' I pause. I told Hugh, so I know I'm capable of saying it again:

'I also have an eating disorder. Bulimia.' Dr Brinke's face is impassive; he doesn't say anything. 'But I don't know if that is the problem or if something else is the problem and that is just the result.'

With relief I see Dr Brinke nod very slightly. Perhaps I'm making some sense. So I forge on: 'I suppose I could just be depressed and the bulimia is a symptom of that depression, or the bulimia is causing all of these other ramifications, like feeling depressed. I suppose I'm not managing very well in general,' I say. Dr Brinke stays quiet. 'At least, I don't think I am.' Dr Brinke nods once, so I continue:

'I'm tired, my mood swings up and down, I don't feel in control, at all. I can't predict how any day will turn out, whether

I'll lose it or not. I'm not in control of things, but I don't know why, or what I can do about it.'

There's a movement from the garden. A cat is peering in short-sightedly from the other side of the glass door. It loses interest and stalks stiff-legged towards the bushes.

'I don't talk to anyone about my eating disorder, or about the other stuff really. My family doesn't know. They know I struggle with depression, sometimes. So that's what I've told them, that I'd like to see you to help with my low moods. My friend Hugh, at college, told me you'd helped someone he knows with bereavement, and that's how I found out about you.'

Dr Brinke adjusts his position in his chair and I realise what I have just said.

'This isn't anything like bereavement, of course.' I shake my head emphatically – I wouldn't want Dr Brinke to think that I was comparing this lack of self-control to anything as terrible as bereavement. 'But . . .' I tail off, look out the window of the study at the tangle of disordered English garden into which the cat has disappeared and I let myself slip into a momentary darkness. What is it that's wrong with me? Why am I here? I am embarrassed to be here. This isn't right for me, sitting and talking about myself. All I need to do is go out and seize life with both hands. I wish Dr Brinke would say something, do something.

I think of the woman in the bakery at the bottom of the hill in Kampala, where they sell the different-coloured pound cakes and loaves of bread, and I think of the shame I felt buying the slab of yellow cake from her when the man in front of me wore poor clothes and misshapen, mended shoes. And then I think of the Kenyan man who stood in front of me on the tube in

London one day. I could tell he was newly arrived from Africa just by his shoes, like the ones the man in the queue in the bakery wore. Real, African shoes, black, with laces, too wide in the heel from so much use but clean and mended. Seeing his shoes and the thinness of his shoulders on the Underground escalator filled me with pity.

I pull myself back into the room. Again, Dr Brinke nods, just a slight tilt of his head. 'The thing is,' I continue, 'I don't really know what the problem is, or even if there is a problem or if it's all . . .' I can't find the word. 'Imaginary' is one word that might fit, but it's not quite right. I wait for Dr Brinke to respond. He doesn't seem ready, maybe he is thinking.

I look down at my hands. I can't understand why I can't shake it off, why I can't stop it. Even when I was in Madrid, some months back, it carried on, unchecked. I liked Madrid, I liked my Spanish housemates, I made friends, went to classes, explored the city, spoke Spanish, had boyfriends. Men propositioned me at traffic lights and in the park. A stranger in a business suit asked me to join him for lunch as I waited to cross the road at a junction in the north of the city.

But I also kept the other life going. I replaced custard creams with Príncipe Lu biscuits and the yellow cake fingers filled with chocolate you find in Spanish supermarkets, four in a row, under plastic, and *napoletanas* and *magdalenas* from a cheap bakery near the Parque Berlín. It just helped. It filled in the time between classes and other things going on. It filled it all out. Each time I bought the yellow cake fingers I pictured well-dressed schoolchildren all over Spain dipping them into hot milk at breakfast, leaning neat side partings over their mothers' kitchen tables.

I stayed up late at night to finish off the business once my housemates had gone to bed. I had my own bathroom on the ground floor, next to the kitchen; my housemates' rooms were all upstairs. Still, I ran the shower at the same time, to hide the sound, just in case.

What on earth is wrong with me? I look back into Dr Brinke's garden. I could easily lose myself in this dark moment. I feel pulled towards the shaded ground between Dr Brinke's garden wall and the tangle of climbing roses where I can see browning leaves on dark soil. I wonder what Dr Brinke is thinking, quietly, behind his desk. I wonder where the cat has gone.

'Well,' Dr Brinke says at last. 'Why don't we start with your family? Why don't you tell me about your family?'

This is good. An easy warming-up kind of beginning. If only he'd started with that in the first place. My family is unconnected to this. Dr Brinke is helping to put me at my ease. I'm glad he seems to be taking control of the direction of this, perhaps we'll move more fluidly to the heart of things from here.

'My family lives in Uganda,' I say. 'In Kampala, the capital. They moved there two months ago from Ethiopia. My father works for the World Food Programme, which is the food and logistics agency of the United Nations, set up to respond to humanitarian emergencies. Famines, civil wars, displaced refugee populations, and so on.' I realise I'm sounding like my father. This is probably unnecessary detail for Dr Brinke, so I tie it up: 'And we've always lived in Africa, mostly, apart from a few years in Pakistan.'

Dr Brinke doesn't move, he's still and expressionless behind his desk and his large round glasses. He must think that wasn't sufficient.

'My mother doesn't really work other than looking after the family and the house and taking care of things. She's very warm and kind. Well, so is my Dad. I have a close family. My brother has finished university, he's working in Ethiopia. I think he's working on a wild dogs conservation project now, or perhaps that was his previous project, I'm not sure.'

Still no reaction from Dr Brinke. Perhaps he thinks wild dogs are just domestic dogs that have gone wild – like the ones that roamed around in packs in Khartoum, scavenging around the rubbish dumps – not a species of endangered wild animal. I think of William in some arid landscape of eastern Ethiopia clunking around in an old Land Rover looking for wild dogs. A passing urge to explain to Dr Brinke about wild dogs dissipates.

'And my sister is at Sussex University. She's just a year older than me. We're close but I suppose we don't see that much of each other now that we're both in England. We see each other sometimes, though.'

There's a clock on the wall above the desk, above Dr Brinke. The minute hand shifts one increment to the right.

'So my family is fine,' I say.

Dr Brinke doesn't say anything for a few moments. I think I see his head nodding, very slightly.

'The family is fine,' he says, finally.

'Yes,' I say, waiting for the next question, but the next question isn't forthcoming. It occurs to me that Dr Brinke might be casting doubt on what I've just said, about the family being fine. Or it may be that he wants to know more about them. But in the quiet wash after the last words, I find myself doubting.

Isn't the family fine? Is it possible that my family, my upbringing, the events of our family life are connected to this illness?

That the way we are is implicated in some way in the predicament I find myself in now? That the way I am is a result of the
way we are, the way we look at things, the way we do things?
There it is, a simple enough question, but it brings with it a wash
of such ashamed disloyalty towards my parents, my siblings, my
upbringing in Africa, towards the man with the mended shoes
and the young woman selling pound cakes, that I shake the
thought away. I don't need to think about that.

No, this comes from within *me*, from some brokenness within
me, unconnected to other people or to my relations with the
world. This is my problem. I created it and I perpetuate it. It is
a simple causality. If x, then y. If I stopped doing it, then the
problem would go away. So I am the problem. It has no existence
in any dimension other than my own orbit of control. Because
as Dr Brinke will, I'm sure, come to understand, the truth is
that I've been given every advantage in life. I've dug myself into
this hole with no outside help. The problem is inside me, but
what that problem is is hard to define. This is why I'm here, to
find out.

'The family is fine,' I say, and I wait for Dr Brinke to speak.

Fourteen

Visit from Oxford to my sister in Brighton.
November 1995

Anna glances into the back of my car. The back seat is covered with discarded food wrappers, an empty fried-chicken box sits sideways on the back seat, the lid caved in, as if it has been kicked there and abandoned. I pretend I don't see her, brown eyes, still face, as she looks back at me, then turns back again to the mess on the seat as I negotiate into a parking space on the seafront, nudging back and forth, back and forth, until I am aligned with the pavement. I pull on the handbrake, breathe out, crossly, as though it was a physical and mental effort to park here, by the seaside.

'There's a lot of rubbish back there, sis,' she says.

'Hmm,' I say. 'I know. I need to give the car a good clean. I'll do it when I get back to Oxford.'

She watches me a second longer than normal, then looks again at the food wrappers, as though she is trying to figure something out. I know she won't guess, nobody has ever guessed.

But I'm surprised myself that I've left so much evidence there for her to see, in this flat midday light. Evidence of something awry, even if she doesn't know what it is. I could have binned it all before I came down to visit.

'Shall we?' I say, and I open my door so a cold wind blows in.

I've come to see Anna for the day at her university in Brighton. I phoned and told her I needed to get away. Low mood, I said. I told her I needed a change of scene. She asked me to come as soon as I could. Now that I'm here I can't shake the mood. I'm finding it hard to pretend to be enthusiastic but I'm doing a good enough job, probably. In some ways it would be easier to be back at Oxford, unaccountable to family, unaccountable to anyone, really. I'll leave as soon as we've had our walk on the beach.

We climb the steps down towards the pebbles, then head on towards the sea. We stand looking out for a moment, watching the perpetual energy of the waves crashing and crashing towards us. Straight over there is France, so this body of sea is a channel, an arm of sea, an arm of the Atlantic. I wonder what kind of northern French beach we'd emerge onto if Anna and I decided to swim over.

'Which way?' I ask. Anna points to our left. I do a mental calculation, picturing the points on the compass. We are facing south, right at the bottom of the island where it widens out like a mollusc foot, so east is the direction we are headed. We start walking fast to warm ourselves, staying as close as we can to the waves, stumbling over pebbles. Seagulls screech and flap about in the wind.

When we reach the groynes, we have to climb up the beach to scramble over them, then we go back down to the waves again. At first we don't talk. We walk and climb and scramble over the pebbles, but soon we're past the groynes and ahead of us is a long stretch of beach. I don't really want to talk about university, I don't really want to ask Anna about hers either. I don't want to feign interest in the mundane detail of daily life, but I know I have to – what else is there to say? We've already covered the broad facts, in her house when I arrived, sitting at the small kitchen table with our cups of tea. She's well, she likes university, she likes her housemates. One of them is Kenyan, and was at our school in Kenya, another is Greek, the other is English. She's in her final year now.

Anna crouches down to pick up a cuttlefish bone, she turns it over to examine it. I see her push her thumbnail into its soft, chalky belly, feeling its consistency. I do that too, with cuttlefish bones. I pick up a handful of pebbles and aim them into the sea. Then we walk fast again. If I can keep walking fast I might shed some of the heaviness of things, the muddiness. Anna holds the cuttlefish bone as she walks.

I look up at the view in front of us, all shades of grey, pebbles and sky, and a pier. A cluster of seagulls fight over a cardboard box, like the one in my car, for the remnants of chips.

'Do you like this beach?' I ask Anna, trying to keep my voice neutral, positive.

'Yes, I do,' she says. 'I love walking down here. Even in the winter. Especially in the winter, funnily enough.'

'You're lucky to live near the sea,' I say to her, still trying to be positive, to keep my head out of the darkness I feel sloshing around in my belly.

The beach is steep here, it would be easier to walk up the pathway with the skateboarders and dog walkers and babies in prams, but neither of us would choose to do that: it's wilder down here.

Anna laughs suddenly. She throws the broken cuttlefish bone down to the waves, it comes back to her on a gust of wind. 'I've just remembered something,' she calls over to me. 'Do you remember when Mum first brought us to boarding school and we went for a walk, the three of us? William must already have been at university. And it was a really crap day, cold, probably, and grey. Like this one. And we were in some bleak field, in winter, and Mum said to us, "I love this watery English landscape."'

I do remember.

'We had no idea what she was talking about,' Anna says. 'I think I probably even wondered if Mum really thought that, or if she was just being positive, for our sakes.'

We reach the pier. We have to scramble up the beach towards the pathway and climb over a wall to get underneath the pier, to get past its giant stilts. Two teenagers sit at the top, in the semi-dark damp of the pier's underside, smoking a joint. We come out the other side, the sun breaks out from a cloud. In the far distance I see waves crashing against a grey sea wall. We clamber back down to the sea, walk as close as we can to the waves without getting too wet.

'Hugh phoned me,' Anna says. 'He said he was worried about you. He said you keep, sort of, disappearing.'

'I'm just busy, I suppose.' I stop suddenly, pick up three pebbles and throw them into the sea.

'And that you're thinking of not continuing with Dr Brinke,' Anna adds.

'That's true.' I reach down for another handful of pebbles.

'I just don't know if he is actually helping at all. It feels so self-indulgent. I mean,' I continue, 'I'm fine really, aren't I? Look at me. I'm fine.' I throw my pebbles into the sea, one after the other, angrily. I aim for what looks like a plastic bag, floating just under the surface just beyond the waves. My stones sink it.

Anna stands next to me, picks up her own pebbles, two of them, and clicks them against each other, thoughtfully.

'Maybe you should stick with it a bit longer. You've only seen him a couple of times.'

'Hmmm,' I say. 'I don't know. I'm going to see him next week anyway.' I look down at my hands, drop my last handful of pebbles onto the beach, there is no point throwing them.

'There's no reason to stop seeing him, is there?' Anna asks. 'Don't you think you should, just in case?'

'In case what?' I say, unhelpfully. 'I just don't think he's helping.'

We keep walking. I march a couple of paces ahead of my sister.

We don't talk for some time. I don't know what Anna is thinking about. We've come to a long stretch of seaweed. We both crouch down to look at it more closely. At the ends of its fronds the seaweed is swollen into green bubbles. I pick up a strand and squeeze a bubble between thumb and forefinger. It makes a satisfying pop. I wipe my hands on my jeans, dig my fingers into my pockets. I wish I could talk to her, but I don't know how. I would have no idea how to even begin. And there is so much I could say, if I did begin I don't know how I would stop. But I can't say anything, because the one thing I need to tell her, that I am sick, I can't tell her, and it freezes the rest of it inside me.

We walk more slowly now. Anna pulls her thick, curly hair into a knot at the nape of her neck. She links her arm into mine.

'Do you understand now what Mum was talking about?' I ask Anna.

She looks over at me. 'About what?' she asks.

'You know. The watery landscape, or the wintry landscape. Whatever it was she called it.'

'Oh, that,' Anna says. We crunch on over the pebbles, the wind blows around us. 'Yes, I think I do now.'

We pause and I watch the waves, crashing and crashing against the sea wall, a grey spray lifting into the air.

Fifteen

Oxford University. February 1996

I park my car on the street outside Dr Brinke's house and make my way along the side of it and down the garden pathway to his study. I look out for the cat, but he is nowhere to be seen. Dr Brinke is in there behind his desk. He lets me in and I take my place on the sofa, relieved to be here in the peace.

I look at the now familiar paintings on the wall, the books on the shelves: Jung and Freud mainly. I look out again for the cat, who still occasionally stares in through the glass. And all the while Dr Brinke sits silently waiting. This is our fifth meeting so I am getting used to his silence. A still garden. An ordered room. Quiet. A low table in front of me with a white envelope, the bill for the last two sessions, discreet, we don't have to talk about the money. Every other visit the white envelope is there, on the low table, waiting for me. I take it back to college and relay it to my parents in Uganda.

I place my apple on the table top, stalk upward, next to the bill. I'll break the silence or he will, eventually, but I'm so used to his silence now that I no longer feel the need to talk immediately. This peace, this contained and safe quietness, feels precious to me. If I could just hold on to this peace perhaps nothing bad would follow. I could stay within it and push it outwards, a millimetre at a time, and stay here inside it. And so I do for some minutes.

And then the dream comes flitting back to me for the first time in the day. The dream I had at the morning end of sleep will delay the getting into the grit of things, when I'll tell Dr Brinke about all the sordid rest of it, about failing to stay afloat since coming back from visiting Anna last term. So I tell Dr Brinke about my dream.

In my dream I am a leopard and I'm down by the riverbank in the deer park. I can see myself from above. It is dusk or dawn and everything around me is in a half-light, but my leopard patterning shines up through the gloom. I'm crouched low against the dead brown leaves and I'm creeping forward, as though stalking prey. In the dream I feel released. Nothing more happens. I stop describing the dream, there is no more to describe. It was just a story really, and it falls into a pool of still silence as I thought it would. But then:

'A leopard,' Dr Brinke says.

'Yes.'

'A leopard is a very special creature,' he says.

'Yes, it is,' I agree. It was always a rare sighting to spot leopard on our travels across the national parks, our dawn game drives. Leopard had the highest points in our game, followed by cheetah and then lion. We scored points for the animals we spotted. My brother usually won; he has always had an instinct for wild animals. I was usually the last to see them.

I used to pray for a special kind of X-ray vision that would tell me where wild animals were. 'Keep your eyes peeled,' Dad would say, as we bumped over potholes, the dawn rising over the escarpment. And as the car filled with the smell of thermos-flask coffee and powdered milk, and the emergency jerrycans of water sloshed about in the back, I'd imagine a layer of skin peeling off my eyeballs giving me extra-sensitive, animal-spotting vision.

And then there was the leopard who took the neighbours' dog. The neighbours who lived further away, down the dirt track of Ololua Ridge. I swear I saw that leopard; I saw its tail through the window of my bedroom, hanging down from the roof of our house, twitching.

'Do you think you are like a leopard?' Dr Brinke asks me. 'A special creature?'

'No! No, I don't think that at all,' I say. I wish I hadn't told him about the dream, it was just a dream but somehow I seem to have inadvertently revealed that I think I am special.

'No, I don't think that.' I say it again.

But there I am, a white envelope on the table in front of me, an English garden outside, a therapist who is suggesting that I'm telling him I think I'm special. And the man with thin shoulders on the London Underground comes back to me again, and the naked man who carries a boulder on his head on the dusty streets of Addis Ababa near the football stadium. I look at Dr Brinke, the garden light reflecting off his glasses, and I feel a surge of rage against him, against myself. Rage that he won't talk, just talk, like a normal person, and help me, help me in a practical way. Rage at myself for being here at all. No, I'm not a leopard down by the riverbank, I want to shout – I am spoilt, incapable of appreciating all that I have. And the truth is that I'm here because I must think I am special, when really, in the hierarchies of suffering on the planet, mine is as insignificant as a speck of dust. I feel ashamed. This is what I should have told Anna on the beach, that I am ashamed.

I look out into the garden, fighting down my anger, willing the cat to come back, out of the confusion of bushes. I need Dr Brinke to help me in a practical, positive way. This self-analysis is not getting me anywhere. I don't want his silence. This isn't about delving into the past, or about apportioning significance to a dream about a leopard. This has surely to be a question of self-discipline, of pulling myself together, and what I need from him is for him to help me do that.

I leave the apple, stalk up, on the table. I drive my car back down the Banbury Road. Past the hospital and the Taylorian library, past the Bodleian and the Radcliffe Camera. I am still rushing from my anger against Dr Brinke, against myself for getting myself into this situation in the first place. It can't be that hard. I can do this myself. I am the one in control here, am I not? Who else is in control if I am not?

I pass Blackwell's on Broad Street and reach the outer wall of Magdalen College along Longwall Street. Yes, I am in control, I tell myself.

I indicate left. Evening traffic flows around me, lights on, cannot touch me. I radiate power and competence. I turn right opposite the college down Rose Lane. There's a little-known parking space at the end of the lane that leads to the Botanic Garden. It is free. Car in first gear, handbrake on. I get out. I stride down the lane towards the porters' lodge, head up. Everything is going to go my way, I can feel it. I cross the road to Magdalen College and enter the lodge. I will do this. I will take it one step at a time, be practical, be methodical.

I check my pigeonhole for post. I walk smartly across the first quadrangle, under the archway, past the chapel, through the Cloisters, across New Building's lawns, and unlock the door to the staircase at the far corner; three more paces and I am at my front door. I place my letters in a pile on the desk, corners aligned, and pick up the telephone. I dial Dr Brinke's number. I know he won't answer because he has a visitor immediately after me. I thank Dr Brinke for his help and tell him I don't feel I need to come back in the new term.

I am brimming with resolve.

Sixteen

I'm in the supermarket on Cornmarket gathering food. I'm at the refrigerated section with the cream cakes, cheese-cakes, chocolate and whipped-cream sundaes, double slices of chocolate cake nose to nose in pretty boxes, pinked, floral, labelled with curled and feminine lettering. If only all these could be mine, every one of them mine, end to end, unending. I can't take my eyes off the shining thick velvety chocolate frosting, peaking and swirling and spilling around the moist darkness of cake, and my mouth fills with saliva, my cheeks and tongue and head ache with longing. One of these I can have, but which one, and which do I leave behind? One will never be enough. I want to dive into a never-ending flow from a magic porridge pot, I want to gobble up the Hansel and Gretel house in the forest, I want to scrunch into the whole roast boar like Obelix at the feast, over and over and over again.

An easy flow of shoppers moves around me but I am unmoving. Do it. Make a decision. This one. I'll have this one. I hold it and claim it. I move on to the next section.

Perhaps that's where she saw me. And then I suppose she took her time, followed me around the shop as I chose items and put them, some into my bag, some into the wire basket. Two cream cakes, shortbread and a pot of custard in my bag, the rest placed in the wire basket, conspicuous, honest. I paid for the milk and the marshmallow biscuits, I paid for the flap-jack, the loaf of bread and the rich chocolate layer cake on offer – round, almost the size of a real cake.

Or perhaps she wasn't physically there. Perhaps she spied me there at the cream cakes on a security camera – the girl frozen by the Hansel and Gretel house, while others flowed around her – and watched, switching to different cameras as I moved about the store. Before I left the shop, twenty paces before the auto-matic doors and the security guard in uniform, alongside the rails of sensible older women's clothing, the cardigans and tapered trousers and scarves, I tore open the marshmallow bis-cuits, and was eating them quickly, hungrily, stuffing down my fear as I stepped into the street.

One, two, three, four, five paces down the street, and there she is. A woman I don't know. She appears at my side and then stands in front of me. She has a radio in her hand. Can you come with me, she says. This way, she says. There's someone else there. A male security guard, perhaps. I keep eating. I eat to hold on, to bury it, but I know it's too late. And stop eating that, for God's sake, she hisses at me. Confused, I hold the biscuit out to her. She looks angry, disgusted, and points at my plastic bag. In there, she says. I drop the half-eaten marshmallow biscuit back into the plastic bag, it settles amongst the debris of fine foil wrappers.

We return to the store and up some stairs into a small room where there is another man, a policeman. He takes all the objects out of my bag and lays them on a table, asks to see the receipts for everything I have with me. I have a receipt for the jacket I bought from Topshop and the book from the second-hand section upstairs at Blackwell's, a collection of short stories by Guy de Maupassant in English. I should be reading it in French.

He separates out the cream cakes, the shortbread and the pot of custard. These items are not accounted for on the receipt. He places them at one end of the table.

She is still there and she seems to get angrier as the policeman does his inventory. Perhaps she mistakes my silence, my shock, my fear, for insolence and hates me for it. Perhaps she has other things to despise me for too. She wouldn't even stop eating when I arrested her, I can imagine her telling her husband that evening as she takes off her sensible shoes in the hallway, sensible shoes for catching robbers.

'Can I please talk to you alone?' I say to the policeman.

'Yes,' he says. He asks her to leave. She looks at both of us before she leaves the room.

I tell him I am bulimic. It's an eating disorder, I explain. And I'm taking the food because . . . Because I'm owed it? Because I don't want to pay for it? Because I'm a thief? Because it's part of the disorder to get lots of food and eat it. I don't know why I'm telling him this. I'm trying to be honest, but it's too late for that now.

'The thing is that I'm trying to get help,' I say. 'I even saw a therapist, I'm sure he . . .'

'OK,' he says. I think it's kindly. 'But I'll still have to take you down to the station.'

She comes back in.

'I'm taking her down to the station,' he says. She nods.

I get in the back of his police car. I lower my head and turn it inward as if I am talking to someone inside the car. I pray nobody sees me.

I sit on the bed in the cell. The door shuts and bolts. I look down at my feet on the floor, align them side by side, socks touching. What I was carrying with me has been taken away and placed in a plastic bag, along with my shoes, for me to collect later. There is nothing now to buffer me, nothing to stop me facing up to where I am and what I have done. Any minute now I'll have to look over the edge; there's no stopping it and I know it. Right foot. Left foot. They are my grandmother's small feet. But I don't recognise them here, they look strange. Nonetheless, they are mine. I think of my grandmother's doll-sized shoes in the cupboard next to her bed. I wish we had kept them after her death although they were half a size too small for me, and so we let them go.

I hear two people laughing and footsteps down the corridor; I imagine the sound reflecting off the outside of the metal door. The paint on the metal door is worn away in places. The square of metal grille is speckled with paint of a different colour, a colour it was once but is no longer supposed to be. I'll be sent down from Oxford. But that is nothing, compared to the other thing: I'll have to tell. I'll have to tell my parents what I've done. My family will know. My friends will know too. I will be pulled out of my hiding place, it will be opened and torn about and it won't even be my decision. They will all know about me.

I cover my face with my hands and cry with a deep, hoarse, animal kind of cry. The crying wipes everything out, everything outside itself. I fall into it; I don't want it to end. When it ends I know I will be back here again, where I am, sitting on a bed in a cell.

When the crying stops, I lie down, close my eyes, and wait.

'Would you like a cup of tea?' says a voice. There is a portion of face looking in at me through the grille.

'Tea. Yes, please,' I say, rubbing my eyes.

'Milk and sugar?'

'Yes, thank you.' He goes away. I stand up and look out through the grille. I see his back walking away from me. He reappears quickly, with my tea in a small Styrofoam cup. And then he goes away again.

I drink the tea sitting on the bed. I have to be strong, but I don't know if I know how. I just have to deal with this now, now that it has happened. I already know some of what will follow. One of the policemen who took my statement told me that I will be sent down from the university, but because I'm older than eighteen, he also said, my parents will not be informed of my arrest, so it is up to me to tell them, to explain.

I will just have to think of a way of telling.

The door opens and I'm asked to follow a policeman back to the room where they took my statement.

'We're letting you go now,' he says. 'You're lucky – we're giving you what's called a "formal caution". A formal caution means you're on our books, but it's not the same as a criminal record because it expires in four years' time if you don't reoffend. If you reoffend it will be more serious. So just don't do it again.'

I wonder if I'm supposed to say thank you. Instead, I nod.

'And when you get back to college you'll have to go and see the President, he's waiting for you. The police who searched your room had to get permission from the President of the college because Oxford University colleges are private land,' he explains. He sounds put out. 'So you'll have some explaining to do, no doubt.'

'Did they have to tell him what it was for?' I ask.

'No. That's a matter between you and us. So as I say, you'll have some explaining to do.'

I collect my things. It's dark, and I'm glad of the darkness.

In the warm light of the porters' lodge, the head porter tells me I can go straight to the President's lodgings. I cross the first quadrangle. It's a clear night, I can see stars. Lamps glow gently in the ornate stone windows of the President's home. Tonight the college seems soft, mild. I take a deep breath and ring the bell. I've been once before, to the President's Lodge. We were all invited to dinner here, in our first year. We drank port and the President showed us paintings and ancient manuscripts. Wilfred Thesiger comes here, I know that. I know my brother has met him, I think my father has too, in Ethiopia. Wilfred Thesiger. Oscar Wilde. They've both been here and left their mark.

The President's assistant opens the door and leads me to a room with a desk, pools of shadow falling across it, and invites me to sit down. Then they both reappear and sit opposite me. The assistant sits off to the side, in shadow. The President leans forward, his hands on his knees, looking embarrassed. The lamp light filters through stray grey hairs on his head and gleams off his large round glasses.

'I understand you were arrested,' he says, with an awkward smile.

'Yes,' I say. 'I'm sorry.'

'What happened?' he asks.

I know what I have to say but the thought of it sickens me. I have no choice.

'I was shoplifting,' I say. 'It was a stupid thing to do.' And then I lie. 'It was a prank, really. And I'm sorry. I know it was stupid.'

He looks relieved. He is still smiling in the same way, his cheeks looking full and young in spite of the grey hair. He seems to be attempting to show support, solidarity. Strange, as he must be about to ask me to leave.

'Right,' he says. 'Well, I suppose you aren't going to do it again, not after all this fuss.'

'No,' I say. I try to smile back. I really do feel sorry, very sorry. I wish I could have left a better mark, like Wilfred Thesiger.

'Right. Well, you can go now, if you like.'

'Go?'

'Yes,' he says. 'Unless there's anything else you, er, wanted to discuss, that is.' He looks nervously at his companion, hoping this isn't the case.

'But aren't you . . . I thought you were going to send me down.'

'Good Lord no,' he says. 'After all, we've all been in trouble like this at some stage or another. It would be a strange thing if we hadn't.' He smiles at me and at his assistant, inviting us to concur. Then he laughs, his assistant laughs too, both relieved and embarrassed in equal measure.

* * *

I close my bedroom door, lean my back against it, close my eyes and offer a prayer of thanks. I stay that way, eyes closed, sheltered in a reddish womb of dark, and breathe. I am alone. I am safe again. In one hand my bag, with my book, my new jacket, in the other the plastic bag from the supermarket.

The room is quiet, secure, wooden window frames, old radiators. There it is, my succulent plant in its clay pot, the desk in the corner, small fridge humming. It is all still there. I left the room tidy this morning and it is still that way, in spite of everything. I put down the bags and walk through the living room into my bedroom. My bed is made, neat. I walk back into the living room, sit down at my desk, look around. There is no sign that two policemen searched my room earlier.

I hang my jacket in the cupboard, place Maupassant on the desk, then open up the plastic bag. Milk, marshmallow biscuits, a flapjack, a loaf of bread, a chocolate layer cake. The cake has a diagonal dent in its packaging, the icing smeared across the inside of the plastic. The milk carton is wet with condensation and speckled with dark crumbs. At the bottom are the silvery biscuit wrappers, a pale-green foil, delicate, crushed into the corners of the bag. And the debris of the half-eaten biscuit. I remove the milk and hold it over the waste-paper basket as I wipe it clean. I place it on the table. Then I take out the loaf of bread and do the same. There are four remaining marshmallow biscuits from the packet. One by one I clean off the crumbs and place them on a small plate. They are wrapped, contained, edible as individual entities; they can be safe foods. I can offer them to other people. I'm not sure what to do with the chocolate cake; it is messy, dangerous, extreme. I'll give it away, I'll leave it in the communal kitchen with a note saying 'Eat me'. Then I crumple the bag with its debris and put it in the waste-paper basket. I place the milk, white, clean, into my fridge, and next to it the bread and the flapjack.

There's a knock on the door. I move the chocolate cake out of sight before going to open it. It is my friend Hugh.

'Oh, thank God you're here,' he says. 'I had no idea what happened to you.'

I let him in. He's too nervous to sit on the low mattress by the table. He perches on the side of my desk.

'I came here at lunchtime and found two policemen searching your room. They wouldn't tell me what was going on. They wouldn't even tell me if you were all right. Can you believe it? What on earth happened? Are you OK?'

'I'm fine,' I say. 'I've had a really crap day. I was arrested.'

I already know what I'm going to say. I thought of this on my way back to college, knowing I would have to come up with something, anything. Not the truth, not even to Hugh, who knows about my habit. And so I tell Hugh a story, a lie about being arrested for buying dope from a friend I bumped into in town. A Kenyan friend he doesn't know.

'I had to give a statement,' I say. 'And now I have a formal caution.'

Hugh is staring at me. 'I thought you might have died,' he says. 'I'm sorry.'

'At least they could have told me you were OK. What's the point in not even telling me that?'

Once I've answered Hugh's questions about the incident I run up the cold staircase to the second floor and fill the kettle from the sink in the bathroom. I make us both a cup of tea.

'Biscuit?' I hold out the plate to Hugh, he takes one.

He opens the foil wrapper and eats the biscuit, absently. At Hugh's house, a beautiful manor house in Oxfordshire, they have tea every afternoon. His mother brings it out on a tray with delicate teacups and saucers. There is always a cake and chocolate from a biscuit tin, and crumbly biscuits in old-fashioned packaging that look like they were made in an English kitchen. They eat without any discernible greed, the family, neglectfully almost. Thin, restrained slices of cake. One, perhaps two biscuits, nothing more. Tea is poured carefully, just a thoughtful splash of milk. Beyond the sloping lawn and the ha-ha, sheep amble in a farmer's field.

That night I pray. I close my eyes and lower my head and close my hands underneath my chin. I decide then that once I have finished my degree I will leave England and return to my family in Uganda. I will tell my family about my problem, and with a clean slate, in a different environment, I will start again. I stay beside my bed, kneeling, my head lowered, my eyes still closed.

I haven't prayed like this since we went to church as children, bumping down the drive, turn right and along the dirt road, my mother's bangles chiming against each other, the wind blowing into the car from over the long grass, the tall trees; and beyond the trees the wind coming down over the Ngong Hills, messing up my brother's hair, brushed into a side-parting like Dad's, for church, and my sister and I with shined shoes too big for us – they were bought in the summer holiday in England and would have to last us all year.

'*Riega mi alma con tus lágrimas!*' Dad would call out to us. He'd be standing in the high yellowing grass of the garden, waving. It means 'Water my soul with your tears'. Dad doesn't believe in God, not the kind of God you have to go to church to pray to; he would say it to make Mum laugh, and also because it sounds beautiful in Spanish. He'd come to church at Christmas, though. 'For your mother,' he'd say.

Mum does believe in God. She went to a Catholic convent boarding school, and she loved it there. She loved the nuns and the music and the ritual, and the teachings and the stories. She'd pray for us every night just before bed, making a small sign of the cross on our foreheads before she began:

Jesus of Nazareth
King of the Jews
Preserve you from a *suddenan'unprepared* death . . .

We'd lean on the windows, waving and calling to the dogs chasing us down the drive, kicking up dust, barking. Even the little rain we'd had there, towards the south of the country, would not have reached the farmers and the nomads in the north. They'd still be waiting for rain for their maize and their cattle. We drive slowly, hoping to see the giraffe, hoping the giraffe will make us late for church.

God Bless you
Guardian Angels look after you
Amen.

Then another sign of the cross on our foreheads.

In church, I would try to see God. As the drumming filled the church to its corners, I would focus my attention on a thick pillar candle on the wooden table at the front, on the puffs of dark smoke that came out of the flame and floated to the ceiling. Was that God? Maybe that was Him giving me a sign. Or maybe it was the Holy Spirit. I imagined the Holy Spirit looked a bit like that, wispy and floaty, like the smoke that came out of the candle. But as I watched the candle I'd see more puffs of dark smoke and become suspicious. I didn't think it was meant to be that easy to see God. Maybe it was just a puff of smoke after all.

I pray now, in my room at Oxford, and again I try to feel some connection with God, but nothing comes back. I pray when I am struggling, and sometimes I remember to pray in a simple kind of way, in my bed at night, even when I don't need anything, because I like the feeling it gives me, of humility, of the spaces of calm I can feel opening up in my head like still pools of water. And even though I'm not sure anyone is listening, I don't think it matters, because it helps. It always helps. In the feeling of surrender, in the humility of giving up, I find a momentary peace.

India, 1993.

PART IV:
AFRICA
1999–2000

The day we leave Ethiopia for Lesotho, 1976.

Seventeen

Uganda, 1999. Twenty-four years old

I twist the handle and push up the garage door of the house on the hill, in England. The door swings open, creaking. I like the smell in here. It reminds me of the summer holidays we used to have here when we were little, of British bulldogs on the green. I can see some of my brother's boxes in here, and Anna's, against the back wall. William works in Kenya now, Anna is in Uganda; so they have both packed up their English boxes and moved on. I'll add mine to theirs, against the back wall, cardboard boxes full of the belongings I've packed up from Oxford. I've kept my textbooks and essays and exam papers, my degree certificate: I doubt I will ever look at them again, but they are satisfying evidence that I finished. In the other boxes are my winter clothes, my bedspread and mugs and cushions, the kettle I had in my room. I've rolled up my rugs and tied them with rope. I stack them there too, on top of the boxes.

On the plane I wrap my shawl around me and lean my head against the window. I stir the powdered milk into my tea. In the normal way I love flying. I love the fact that for a brief time there is nowhere else I can go. But on this journey I feel heavy and reluctant. I am going to have to be honest, when I arrive, with my family. I am going to have to tell them what has really been going on, which is the same as admitting that I have been lying to them, all these years. That I am not who they think I am – I have lied to them about who I am and what I do. I'm not sure what is left, once you take away what I was before, and what I have pretended to still be: the vigorous, free person doing handstands in the shallow end. I'm not sure what it leaves behind, if we take that away.

I unpack my suitcase as soon as I arrive home, place my books on my side table next to the vase of garden flowers, and hang my clothes in the cupboard. Then I push the empty suitcase under the bed, against the wall where I can't see it, so all I can see is the simple room: a swept floor, a large window looking into the garden, a mosquito net tied in a loose knot over the single bed on which I now sit. A clean slate. This is what I wanted. I wanted to leave everything behind, and start again.

It takes me a week to build up the courage to tell, and every day leading up to telling has required an effort to stay balanced. I have not managed to fully escape the anxiety of what I do; it's there, and I dip in and out of it in unguarded moments. I go to the kitchen and open the door to the pantry, I stand before the shelves and do a mental tally of the food that is in there, should I need it: the packet of plain digestives, the packet of salty crackers, the loaf of bread. The tins are no good, the branch of bananas, the giant jackfruit with its spiky skin, the tin of powdered milk. But I have some shillings in the drawer by my bed – so I know I can always go down to the bakery near the newspaper offices where I am going to take my CV and ask for work. The bakery where they sell the different-coloured pound cakes. I've been tense since I arrived, knowing that I have to tell my family, that this is my plan and I have to stick to it.

I look at them here and see, with a clarity that has eluded me for a long time, how separate we are. There might as well be a wall between us, because they don't know about me and have never known. All they see is a surface layer, a phenotype, but not the rest of it. And even what they do see is untrue because it is based on a premise that has not been true for a very long time: that I am healthy, and normal. I resent them for not knowing, for not being able to see. I decide that it is significant, their not knowing, that it is a wilful blindness on their part. That all they want to see is the positive; that nothing else, in this family, is good enough. But I know that I'm thinking this way because I am afraid.

And then I know that I can't put it off any longer. I have to tell them before William returns to his game reserve in Kenya; I want to tell them all together at the same time. It is a Sunday morning; we are all at home. Dad is the first person I see. I ask him if he would mind asking the others to come to my room. There is something I have to tell them.

I sit on the bed, waiting. I touch the soft swelling of my eyelids. They are puffy, like the turgid parts of a succulent plant. Drip, drip, drip, I can't stop them, tears fall from my chin onto my thighs, squeezing capriciously out of the little holes in my eyelids. Anna discovered the little eyelid holes when we were children, perfect round apertures specially made for the drops to come out. We were amazed. All that time they had been there, and we never even knew it.

The wide branches of the garden trees, dappled through the

mosquito netting over the window, shimmer and dance above my plain wooden desk.

As the four of them enter the room I can't look at them, so I cover my face. The bed dips as my father sits next to me, I feel his hand on my upper arm. It dips again as Mum takes the other side, holds on to my right thigh below my shorts.

'It's OK,' Dad says. 'Whatever it is, we'll help you.'

William and Anna settle at my desk, just across the room from my bed, just two paces away, their backs to the branches of the trees in the garden, which must still be dancing behind them in the early Sunday morning. Clouds are probably building up over Lake Victoria by now, readying for a thunderstorm this afternoon.

They face me, saying nothing. They are very still, and I suddenly realise they must think that I'm dying, that I am going to present them with something terminal and irreversible, something over which nobody has any control. I have to tell them, quickly. I squeeze my eyes shut, focus on switching off that top bit of the brain, the frontal lobe. It's the top of the head, that's the bit I switch off before I dive in. It's the part I have to still before I jump off high rocks into the sea, off the top diving board.

I say it. I describe what it is, and give it its name. My words are in the room and I know there is no going back now. So I keep talking. I open my eyes but keep them fixed on my white shorts, on a frayed patch with a white thread poking out over a freckle at the top of my thigh. I tell them what it means, that I eat a lot, and then I make myself vomit.

I can't bear to see their faces. I don't want to think what they will make of this, what my father in particular must think of this loss of control, of this excess, and what he will think after this.

But I have to keep going now. I tell them I have been doing it for a long time, since I first arrived in England at boarding school, and that over time it has grown into something that is beyond my control, that happens all the time and that I can't stop. I don't mention the arrest. Some things they don't need to know.

Drip, drip, drip. The front of my shorts is damp. I press my finger into the material, I want to see if I can push right through it if I push hard enough.

'I'm not in control at all,' I say, finally. My words sound odd to me, unnatural, as if I'm reading from a script, from something somebody else has written. But now they know. After all this time, they know. It is no longer my secret.

I look up. I keep my hands over my mouth. I hear the sound of my breathing: in, out, in, out. Curious, it all seems the same. I don't know what I expected to see. The trees are still there beyond the mosquito netting on the windows. There's a line of ants on the floor, by the wall, proceeding in single file towards the window. My brother and sister are smiling. My mother is nodding, Dad is squeezing my arm. They are all saying things, but I can't take it in. They are relieved that I am not dying, that I don't have AIDS, that I haven't killed someone or let someone die; they are saying that they can help me, that I am brave. What they mostly feel is relief. I am disconcerted. I'm not sure that I have delivered what I wanted to say, in the way that I wanted to say it. But I can't do it again.

I feel myself separating from the room, as though I am looking down on the scene from elsewhere. And from the corner of my eye I watch the line of ants reach the far wall and begin to scale it, heading for a small hole by the netting over the window that leads out into the garden.

Eighteen

A few months later. Uganda, 1999

Down there in the valley below us, though we can't see it for the profusion of trees and plants in our tropical garden, and the barbed-wire-topped garden wall tangled with passion-flower creepers, is Lake Victoria, teeming with tilapia and gradually choking under the delicate purple flowers of water hyacinth. The lake gives a different quality to the air here, filled with lake smells and humidity and vegetation. It brings us violent afternoon thunderstorms, which break and end suddenly and leave the red roads that wind down our hill to the main roads of Kampala, steaming and baking back into clay.

Dad has just arrived home from a field trip. He has driven several hours across the country from the border with Sudan in the north, from a refugee camp there, and has a faint suggestion of dust about him, of other places, tingeing the dark-brown hair on his arms. Anna is reading in a cane chair next to his.

Charles the houseboy is baking in the kitchen. Since he started his weekly cookery lessons he has taken to making star-shaped biscuits. He bakes them in the oven and they curl up brownly at the edges. They are simple and dry, made with flour and water and sugar, and just one drop of vanilla essence. On the days when he bakes them he'll bring out a plate of the curled brown stars with our afternoon tea on the veranda, and take a plate to the day guards as well. Mother is teaching him to cook. He copies the recipes carefully, in pencil in case he makes a mistake, into a lined exercise book which he keeps on the window ledge in the kitchen.

Charles comes out to us on the veranda, balancing a tray with a teapot and cups, and the plate of biscuits. He places the tray on the low glass-topped table, then straightens up and takes a step back. He tells us he is ready to go home, unless we need him for anything else. Because Dad is here he is more reserved than usual, more deferential. Dad and Charles are not often here at the same time, as Dad is usually back when Charles has already left. Dad leaves the management of the staff to Mum. At the end of each month she sits at the table in the open dining room and the people working at the house come to her, one by one. She goes through their salaries and gives them their money in an envelope; she asks about their families and their health and the school fees. She asks about Charles's second wife who has just had their sixth child, a girl, and his brother who is sick with malaria.

Charles looks too young to have six children, eight if you count the two who have come from the village to live with them. All of them are girls. They live in a two-roomed house not far from us on Mbuya Hill, at the bottom of our hill and further west towards Bugolobi Market. He can walk from our house to his in forty minutes, avoiding the winding road and taking the narrow footpaths that cut down the hill, alongside the barbed-wire-topped fences of the big houses.

We say goodbye to him, we won't see him again until Monday. He returns to the kitchen over the wooden floors, which he polishes every week by balancing barefoot on a large cloth and shuffling from one end of the room to the other until they shine.

Mum places the strainer on the first cup and pours the tea from the pot in a sparkling brown curve of liquid. She passes the cups around. Dad holds his in his strong right hand, takes a thoughtful sip, then holds it still just a few inches above his safari trousers.

'I've been thinking about what you told us,' he says to me. Anna puts down her book and looks up. 'And it occurred to me that what we need is a formula. Some formula that helps us to keep all the important things in balance, those things that contribute to good health and happiness.'

The roar of an engine drifts up from the valley, a distant swell of noise, of industry down at the port. The lake is so vast it is more like an inland sea, lapping at Tanzania over the water, and Kenya to the south and east of us.

'We need a formula that reminds us, easily, what those things are,' Dad says. 'So on the drive back from Gulu I've been trying to come up with an acronym that fits, something we can easily remember. Something that represents all the elements that make for a well-balanced life.'

I take up the long banana basket and offer it around, then choose a small, sweet one. I twist it carefully off its stem and peel down its thin skin. I'm not sure about this formula, something in me is closing against it already. I can't think that a formula would work for me, somehow, but I know I'm being unreasonable.

'And what are the elements of a balanced life?' Dad continues. He holds up his left hand. 'For me, they are Diet. Exercise' – he counts each one off, finger by finger – 'Friends. Organisation. Environment.' All five fingers of his left hand are standing in the air.

'We need all these things and we need them all to be in balance. We need a good diet, plenty of exercise, we need friends, we need to be organised and we need to live in the right environment, the one that suits us. Perhaps there are others we can think of. But above all, of course, and the most important of all is Positivity. Being Positive is absolutely crucial to all of this. In fact, I'd say it's the most important one of all.'

'Allen,' my mother says. 'Sorry to interrupt but aren't you supposed to be playing squash with William Kalema at five?'

'Yes. What time is it?'

'It's five to five,' Mum says.

Dad leaps to his feet, places the cup on the cane table. 'Let's continue this later, if you like,' he says. Then he brings one strong hand down onto my shoulder and the other onto my sister's.

'Aren't we lucky to have such beautiful daughters?' he says to Mum. Then he jogs through the living room and out of sight.

Two turacos flap across the garden.

'Do you think this is helpful?' Anna asks me. 'Coming up with formulas and that kind of thing?'

'I don't know,' I say. 'I'm not really sure what's helpful.'

'I think you need to tell us how to help you, when you've thought about it, of course. If there's anything you can think of, you just need to tell us.'

'I know,' I say. 'Thanks.'

I jump up and cross to the computer, at a desk at the other

end of the veranda, and start the slow process of dialling up for the Internet. Anna and Mum disappear into the house, so after a moment I close down the dial-up and go back to my seat. I watch the garden for birds. I picture the formula taking shape on Dad's journey home, in some vast open space perfect for thinking, at the wheel of his Africa-specification Land Cruiser with its two fuel tanks, two spare tyres and long-range radio antenna swinging at its front, returning from his field trip to the north of the country, from the refugee camps on the border with Sudan. The map is on the passenger seat. The miles of African scenery, red roads, acacia trees, then banana palms as he journeys further south, the sun arcing mightily overhead. I see a trail of dust lifting out from the back of the car as the day turns golden and then red. Dad's left hand resting on the steering wheel, his right elbow resting on the open window, the skin of his arm turning darker and darker as the day deepens.

Everything has changed and everything is the same. It didn't all disintegrate when I told them. I feel the tremors of it, though, when it comes up, of the baring of the truth, the humiliation. But it didn't all fall apart. In fact, there is a softness, a clearer air, in the spaces between us. This is what I feel.

Things did not fall apart. There was no tearing up of the family script. And they have not asked if I have had any bad days in the time that has elapsed since I told them about the problem. I do not want them to ask this question. The euphoria of telling lasted for a few days, but I *have* had bad days since then. I've been back to the woman selling yellow pound cake in the bakery at the bottom of the hill, I have stolen biscuits from the pantry cupboard and hidden them in the drawer of my bedside table, I have stayed up late and crept into the dark midnight kitchen to eat what I can find that I don't think will be missed in the morning: six slices of bread from a loaf, half a pack of butter, half a packet of digestive biscuits. It's harder here. I have to fill a bucket with the brown water saved from the bath to flush the toilet, to make sure it all washes away and leaves no trace. And now that they know, I have to be extra careful. I feel myself already turning inward, detaching, doing what I can to carry it on.

Mother returns to the veranda and sits next to me. We are side by side facing the garden. Two casqued hornbills, a mother and baby, fly past the black metalwork that separates us from the escaping light.

'I think there are three babies altogether,' Mum says. 'There's a whole family of hornbills living in our garden. Have you seen them sitting on the side of the car and looking at themselves in the wing mirrors?'

We sit, looking out for the rest of the hornbill family, or the red flash of the turaco wing under the darkening canopy.

'I wish we didn't have those bars over the veranda,' I say. 'Do we have to have them?'

'We do, I'm afraid. The house isn't secure without them.'

The valley below floats up its noise, its promises, the sounds of other lives, a smell of wood fires, of water hyacinth and fish. The promise of other countries just across the water. As the light escapes, the bars grow.

'Would they be less visible if they were painted white?' I ask.

'No, funnily enough the least visible colour is black,' Mum says. 'I've seen houses with white bars, and it's very hard to see past them. You do get used to them, though. You'll see, you won't notice them as much as time goes on.'

It's true, you do stop seeing. Like our security guards in the wooden hut by the gate, with their rifles poking out like long grasshopper legs. Kampala has the same problem as Nairobi, one that Addis doesn't have – the widespread problem of armed and sometimes violent robbery, with poverty and the enormous gulf between the haves and the have nots underpinning it all. But I don't see their guns any more, just their faces, their radios, the mugs of tea Charles brings out to them through the day. And I never feel unsafe here, no matter where I go in the city.

Dad reappears on the veranda; white shirt, white shorts.

'So after all that thinking,' he says, holding the head of the racquet against his chest, 'I'm afraid the best I could come up with as an acronym for our formula is "DEFOE", but that doesn't include the P for Positive. Diet, Exercise, Friends, Organisation and Environment. So unless we can come up with anything better our formula can be "Be Positive to DEFOE".'

'That's very good,' says Mum.

I'm not sure what to say.

'Was it Daniel Defoe?' Dad continues. 'I can't remember. I think he wrote *Treasure Island*, was that it?'

'Yes, I think it may have been Daniel Defoe, or did he write *Robinson Crusoe*?' Mum offers.

'I don't know,' I say.

'Right I'd better run,' Dad says. 'Sorry to rush off.' He kisses Mum on the head and jogs towards the kitchen and the back door of the house, where he disappears from view. He'll run past the servants' quarters, the guard post where the night-watchman sits on his stool, through the gate and up the steep driveway and up the hill to where a friend has a squash court in his garden.

'Can you imagine wanting to play squash after driving across the country for eight hours?' I say to Mum.

'And he won't have had any lunch,' Mum says. 'He'll have had a couple of digestive biscuits in the car. That's all he'll have eaten all day.'

It's the time of day when I start to feel hungry, when the fading light and the end of the day stirs a thin, melancholic craving, like the smell of the bitter tealeaves at the bottom of my cup. I eat another banana but it doesn't fill me. I wonder if I will ever stop being this hungry. I place the thin banana skin on my saucer; I lay it gently down, uncreased. I could eat another, or I could make myself a piece of toast, to keep away this hunger. I could settle down to the article I'm trying to write for the paper.

'Shall we go for a walk in the garden?' Mum asks. She stands and smoothes down her long skirt.

We climb down the spiralling steps. I hope that in the darkening garden we might see the chameleons. We rescued them from some children who were throwing stones at them as they clung to a bush on a dry plot. Chameleons are considered bad luck in Uganda, so the children were chasing them away. We lifted the shrivelled creatures, hissing and dusty, into a cardboard box, and released them into a tree in the garden, hoping they might make this their home, but they disappeared almost immediately. In the fading light my mother and I peer up into the branches of the chameleon tree, the fruit rotting by the trunk attracting fat juicy flies, the canopy providing shelter, far from the superstitious children who chased them from their thorny bush. This is surely the perfect environment, the E in DEFOE. But neither of us can make them out.

They have run away.

Nineteen

Kenya, 2000

At the end of a year of living in Uganda, we fly to Kenya to visit William on his game reserve on the Laikipia Plateau. We're in a low-wing Piper, flying low enough to clearly see the animals and the shadows they cast across the yellowing dry-season grass, to see pelts shivering off flies. Giraffe, three of them, bolting from the roar of the small plane's single engine, are galloping, straining their long necks, their shadows stretching and skipping over the earth.

'Reticulated giraffe. What beautiful creatures,' my mother calls out from the co-pilot's seat. We climb away from them, tilt our wings towards them so we have a better view of these animals, the ones we used to see in our Kenyan garden, but they veer away from us, hooves crashing in the dust, three of them abreast now. Then we are past them, our own shadow skimming acacias and scrub and Thomson's gazelles, and termites' clay castles reaching up towards us in the sky.

'Wildebeest. Two o'clock,' says Dad. I'm still straining to see the giraffe, but they have gone. I close my eyes to try to embed the image of them more deeply, more safely, into the folds of my brain. I don't want to forget, but I know that I will one day, that the memory, if it recurs, will seem like a husk, the shed skin of something that once existed. I say goodbye to the giraffe, my giraffe, who exist down there, now, who are, now, slowing and easing back and turning in towards each other, disoriented in the sudden peace.

The Wildebeest are on the horizon. From here it doesn't look like the body of a migration. This group looks like the forgotten tail-end. Heads bowed, kicking up dust, straggly beards: I imagine them fording crocodile-infested water, David Attenborough style, the young and the weak disappearing in a froth of slapping crocodiles' tails and brown churning water, helpless legs pointing skyward. I wonder how many African kids like us watch through a prism of David Attenborough's voice, of Alan and Joan Root's documentaries, telling the stories of the scenes we grew up on, imagining that these films were made for us alone.

Perhaps this group became separated on the trek and are now trying, in their dwindling, tired numbers, to make up for lost time. Heads down, persistent, they trudge on, oblivious to our wings tilting and glinting in the sky above them. But as the plane crests over the escarpment we see before us ribbons of black wildebeest, spread like water tributaries across the plain, all moving south, driven on by instinct.

'The migration of the wildebeest,' Mother says.

They barely register us as we arc high overhead so we can see them, more and more and more of them, all moving with a single purpose towards new grass. It is too much to try to say goodbye to this. Time flows on, rushing over and around and beyond the weary backs of the Wildebeest.

'Laikipia is in that direction,' Dad shouts. I have a view of the back of his head and large black headphones in place of ears. 'Directly northeast,' he points. 'I'd estimate we have about another hour and a half in the air. Soon we'll cross the Mau Escarpment, which is the western edge of the Rift Valley, and fly over Lake Bogoria so we can see the flamingos, then we'll come up over the valley at the eastern edge and up onto the Laikipia Plateau.'

Anna and I look at each other and smile. Then she turns back to her window and leans her chin on her palm, looking out. I wonder what she is thinking; I wonder if she too is trying to say goodbye to Kenya. To our giraffe, the ones who would emerge from the forest at the end of our garden and stand in the dirt track to the road. Sometimes we'd play our recorders to them, standing carefully back from the reach of their long legs.

Kenya is our country. We grew up here. Of all the countries where we might have bedded down, Kenya is where we did it, where we left our roots. We arrived in Kenya in our best aeroplane clothes from the small kingdom of Lesotho in the south of the continent, at the opening of a consciousness that begins at the age of five, and we left as teenagers. And everything since then has been lived, consciously or unconsciously, by comparison. We never went far, apart from Pakistan. Ethiopia and Uganda and Sudan are bordering countries, so Kenya was always there, the other side of Lake Victoria, the lake that gives us our afternoon thunderstorms in Kampala; and heading south from Addis, beyond Arba Minch (*Arba*, 'Forty'; *Minch*, 'Springs'), jump into Lake Turkana and swim south, and there's Kenya again. And Kenya's names: Laikipia, Longonot, Lamu, Thika . . . the names are ours too.

We are coming back for a last visit. In two months' time Anna and I will leave Uganda and return to England, and shortly after that our parents will pack up their furniture and the family belongings: the pictures on the walls, the rugs, the Nigerian pottery, the old school exercise books, the red weighing scales and the cracked plastic lemon squeezer, the VHS copies of *I, Claudius* and *The Year of the Wildebeest*. The cane furniture on the veranda will be sold; it will have no purpose in England. Everything else will be packed into boxes and shipped to Britain, and the house on Mbuya Hill will be empty. On a separate ship, our father's Africa-specification Land Cruiser will make the same voyage to England.

We are leaving East Africa, apart from my brother. He plans to remain here in Kenya, managing the lodge on the Laikipia Plateau with its thousands of acres of wildlife-protected land near Mount Kenya.

Mount Kenya, where my father found a woman freezing to death by a stream. She had gone for a walk from a camp lower down the mountain, setting off in light clothes in the sunshine, and lost her way. That evening two climbers arrived at my father's camp, shaking the tents of the exhausted climbers who had just made it through the vertical bog, pleading for help. The rangers refused to begin the search until morning, but she would already be dead by then. So Dad broke the ice off his socks in the dark, and set off with two other mountaineers, ten paces between each of them, calling her name: Maria. After two hours of clambering over frozen clumps of grass in the pitch-black of the vertical bog, they found her.

I turn back to my window, to the streams of pitiful wildebeest, and watch until even they trickle away to nothing.

* * *

A red and white windsock fills and empties, fills and falls by the side of a dirt landing strip on the horizon. Dad points towards it.

'If there is no windsock and no smoke to be seen' – he turns so we can see his profile, hear him above the roar of the engine – 'look for weaverbirds' nests, which will tell you the direction of the wind. The grey-headed sparrow weaver always nests on the leeward side of trees, to stay out of the wind. Aircraft need to land into the wind, especially on short bush airstrips, like this one.'

We are overhead now, the windsock below us flapping, falling, flapping, falling.

'This is it,' says Dad. 'This is William's airstrip.' And as he speaks we see a Land Rover bumping towards us from the east. William is standing up in the open back, next to Wangesha, his Maasai head guide, waving. We buzz low over them to wave and shout, then turn to come down over the airstrip, buzzing again to clear the game. Several impala are grazing over the landing strip and we scatter them with the engine noise. We turn again to see that two zebra have now wandered across the strip, so we buzz low again. They bolt in small explosions of dust.

'We don't want another ostrich incident,' Mum says, laughing, her eyes bright with the excitement of landing, of seeing William. We come down low a third time to finally clear the strip. The plane roars; the ground looks close enough for me to reach out and touch it.

I drew the ostrich for my school project: instead of a head it had fat red drops of blood spurting out of its neck. It was too late, Dad had said, to do anything but pray that the ostrich would get past in time. It kept running for a long time, even after the tip of the wing had taken its head clean off. The warden in Meru, where Dad landed on his way to a drought-relief programme in Mandera, had the ostrich stuffed and mounted in the hut at the entrance to the park, with a plate underneath that read: 'Ostrich, killed by a bat'. The registration of the Piper Dad was flying was Bravo, Alpha, Tango, BAT.

'All stations Borana, this is Five Yankee Bravo Charlie Echo. We are overhead. Any other traffic? Over.' Just a hiss of static. No other traffic for hundreds of miles.

The field is clear of animals. We come in to land, but just as we touch earth a flock of guinea fowl skims past the cockpit, scattering feathers into the air as we bounce over hillocks, the engine roaring and straining. We slow gracefully, then turn, a suddenly unwieldy bird on the earth.

We bump to the edge of the strip. At the far end of the dirt runway I see my brother climb out of the Land Rover and move quietly towards the injured birds, flapping wings rising and falling over the long grass. I see his arms reach forward into the grass, then the wings are still. He runs back to join us as we climb out of the plane.

That night the five of us sit together to watch a herd of elephant, beautiful, lumbering shapes in the dusk, at the watering hole in the valley below us. I think of the wildebeest, still making their way. A man appears with a basket of wood and stokes up the fire under a vast stone chimney in the lodge. Its flames cast out a flickering light to us as the first stars appear. Soon the sky will be more stars than space.

Usually by now we'd have our own fire going, out in the bush, in the real bush, with our own tents under the stars, just us and a wilderness beyond the light from our campfire. We'd collect sticks before dusk, avoiding baboons, and Dad or

William would build the fire, kindling at the bottom, larger sticks balanced carefully, with plenty of gaps for air to penetrate the heart; the baking potatoes glowing red, foil-wrapped, in the burning coals.

But this wilderness area that William manages, with its mix of wildlife and cattle, is another Africa; this is a luxury-in-the-wild kind of Africa, this one inhabited, sparsely, by white Kenyans, real white Kenyans with Kenyan passports and Kenyan citizenship, who will die here. Not us. We have turned out to be transient.

We watch the elephant, the sky, the large tree, and William talks to us about his life here. Mum makes notes of the birds we've seen in her bird book.

'If we're lucky we might see leopard,' my brother says. 'I've seen a female down there recently.'

I stare down towards the darkening mass of the tree, trying to make out the form of a leopard.

'What's that call?' Mother asks, looking up towards the valley.

William listens for a moment. 'Silver-backed jackal,' he says.

More stillness. The elephants rearrange their ancient tree-trunk legs around the large tree. Their huge forms are fading now into the darkness. The stars, millions of them, bulge out of their galaxies; they look as though they might burst over our planet.

'This is the life,' says Dad.

'This must be very close to paradise,' agrees Mum. 'Do you think so, Willy?'

William hesitates. 'It is, in some ways,' he says. 'It's beautiful, of course, but it's also lonely at times. You'd be surprised how quickly you get used to it, and then even living in paradise has its limitations.'

'Yes,' says Dad. 'You need all things in balance.'

'You need more,' continues William. 'You need friends, of course. But you also need a sense of your own purpose too, and a sense of . . .' – he searches for the right word – 'rooted-ness.' He stands up, looking towards the watering hole. He has seen something. I stare down towards the trees, trying to see the leopard.

'The jackal again,' he says.

'I know I'm lucky to be here,' William says, 'incredibly lucky. But it's not for ever.'

Dad puts his arm around my mother, the bird book is closed on her lap. The watering hole is darkening. William talks to us about the plan he has been working on, late at night in his hut by kerosene lamp, once the guests are asleep. He is planning to set himself up as an African guide and specialist in his own small safari company at whose heart are wildlife conservation and philanthropy. He thinks about it at dawn when he swims before the guests wake.

The valley is now a mass of darkness, but we keep watching, and listening. We don't need to see the animals to know they are there. I look at my parents, next to each other, my father's arm around my mother's shoulders, both watching. They are content; they need nothing more. All our lives we have been taught to revere this kind of wilderness, this kind of paradise. All our lives our parents, and now William, have sought it out – the furthest, the wildest parts of the planet, where there are few others and nothing but a wild beauty, a sky, a fire, a river to swim in, ancient remains in the desert. And here we are, but time flows on, and unless we plant a stick in the ground, and remain, we will leave it behind.

* * *

I try to picture my parents in their sixties terraced house in England. The one with the television set, on the hill where the ice-cream van makes a stop in the summertime. In the town at the bottom of the hill there is a bakery selling a raisined bread called lardy cake, something my father remembered from when he was a child growing up in Suffolk. It surprised me. I had forgotten he had ever belonged anywhere else than Africa.

Mother has somehow retained an Englishness even though she spent even less time than Dad in England before she married, and is half Arab. She was born in Haifa, on Mount Carmel in Palestine, in 1943. With her Palestinian mother and her British army officer father she left Palestine in 1948, just before Palestine became Israel and the Palestinians were driven out. After a few years of army postings in Greece, Singapore and Malaya, the family arrived in England, my mother, aged nine, with her parents and her four younger siblings. They arrived in 1952, on the day King George VI died. Mum was nine years old. As the ship docked at Liverpool, Mum told us, she heard the grown-ups above her head, passing on the terrible news of the death of the monarch. She was bitterly disappointed. She had been so looking forward to coming to England so that she could see a real king wearing his crown.

But Mum has remained connected in some other sense with England. Perhaps it's the simple, practical daily work of our summer visits. The shopping and cooking, and looking after her mother, and buying our clothes for the year in a nearby town. The act of sewing name-tapes into thermal vests and tights which she packed into our school trunks when she eventually settled each of us into boarding school. The merest, most inconsequential actions that turn out to mean you know where you are and how it works.

They won't stay long in the house on the hill, I know. I know they plan to sell and move to a wilder, more rural place in England. But even so I feel a chill of apprehension. I want *them* to have a purpose too. I want them to have a sense of connectedness, of *rootedness*. But take away the connectedness to the earth, the profound outsideness, the smells of woodsmoke or eucalyptus trees in Addis that entrench deeper and deeper, or the clay roads, or the dusty smell before the rain comes, and what is one left with? What is one connected to, ultimately?

Will DEFOE arm *them* in England? Diet, Exercise, Friends, Organisation, Environment. Be Positive. In the depths I fear that I don't believe in the power of DEFOE, not for me. I'm not sure it will ever be enough to dispel an encroaching darkness of mind that I have not shifted, even here, even in paradise. With all my being I wish to believe in its power, for all our sakes.

Our Ethiopian family: Mulu, Wolde and Marta. 1975.

PART V:
ENGLAND
2005

Enugu Relief Staff during Biafra: my parents are middle row,
second and third in from right. 1970.

Twenty

At my parents' home in Sussex. Spring 2005.
Thirty years old

'So your father told me not to stand on ceremony,' Mum is saying, 'and that if I wanted to meet the neighbours we should just invite them round.'

We are walking arm in arm down the country lane next to my parents' home. The lane leads past a beautiful old barn, one of those simply proportioned English farm buildings, soaring and solid and practical, with huge doors and a scattering of farm equipment in its yard. We pause in front of it.

'He's right,' I say. 'You might have to wait another three years if you're waiting for them to invite you first.'

Beyond the barn, the lane runs past a pond with ducks and an ancient oak tree, and beyond that to a fence over which horses hang their contemplative heads.

'Well, we did invite them,' she says, as we continue towards the pond, 'and they all came for a pre-dinner drink one evening. It must have been nearly two months ago. And so far not one of them has invited us back!'

I pull away from her to look at her face and exclaim, but we both laugh. We link arms again and carry on walking. Leading away from this lane are footpaths to walks across country and through woods, and across fields to a village with a church where my sister will one day get married.

'What were they like?' I ask.

We've passed a neat bungalow built close to the lane and with a row of large white-painted stones on the grass verge in front. I don't know what the purpose of it is, of the row of neat white stones. Dad says he must be a colonel, the man who lives there. I wish there were fewer houses in this part of the countryside that my parents have chosen for their home in England, I wish that in place of the houses there were more oaks and ponds and woods and a bleak sort of wildness. And elms and birches and chestnut trees. But Mum likes it like this: she doesn't want to be too far away, too isolated.

'They were perfectly nice,' Mum says.

'Really?'

'Yes.'

We stand at the side of the lane to let the farmer pass in his tractor. The farmer and my mother wave to one another and we watch the tractor rumble on down the lane, away from us. Mum calls for the dog, who has disappeared amongst the farm buildings.

'Wusha ate the farmer's lunch the other day, did Dad tell you?'

'Yes,' I say, laughing. I turn to see the dog reappearing at a run from around the corner of the long, low stables.

'We took round a bottle of wine to say sorry,' Mum continues, though she has already told me this part. 'He was very good-humoured about it – he said Wusha is welcome to his sandwiches any time if he gets a bottle of wine out of it.'

We pause at the pond and peer through the low-hanging branches, looking for the moorhen. On the other side of the pond, between us and the fields, is a solid oak that looks as though it has stood there, as still as it is now, for centuries, and beyond the oak a scattering of sheep dot a gentle hill sloping into the distance. Every detail of the oak is reflected perfectly in the pond's still surface.

'Who knows,' I say to Mum, 'maybe it's a good thing not to know the neighbours too well. After all, they're probably going to be your neighbours for a very long time.'

'Yes,' Mum agrees. 'I'm beginning to think the same.'

The sheep on the hill seem so still today, heads down, attending to the grass with focus and calm, undistracted.

'I can't imagine moving again now. I don't think I'd ever want to,' Mum says.

This surprises me, but I don't respond. I can't imagine my parents being in one place, here, for ever. They are still so young and vigorous. I watch my mother, still peering into the branches looking for signs of animal life, and I am struck by how strong she seems, how settled here, already. She seems unfazed by all the moves, and by this one, which she's saying might be their last move, their last settling-down place. She seems as happy, as unwavering, as she has always been, in all the other places.

'And how's work going?' Mum asks. 'We enjoyed your *Horizon* documentary.'

'Oh good, I'm glad,' I say. 'I didn't think the final outcome was that interesting, but it was a good experience working on it. I like the editor of the strand.'

When I'd had my interview with the editor at the BBC, he

had touched the bald spot on top of his head lightly with his fingertips and warned me that I'd be working with a difficult director. I didn't mind, I'd told him. It was true. The cubicle of his office was cluttered with awards, with posters of volcanoes exploding, a fossil jawbone on a desert landscape, a man in goggles standing next to a particle accelerator. It felt right. This was where I wanted to be. And as an ongoing strand it promised some continuity, some stability, for a while anyway.

There's a sudden splash and we see the moorhen crash into the pond. He speeds across it, leaving two trails in his wake. He vanishes under the trees.

I think back to filming the documentary my mother is referring to. It was a science programme we shot in a remote part of Canada, looking into the neuroscience of religious belief. I think of walking through snow, late one night, to the nearest gas station to buy food supplies for a late-night binge. I remember the lights from the highway and the blinking fluorescent sign in the window of the gas station gleaming softly off the snow. I carried my plastic bag back to the silent hotel. Then, later, when those supplies ran out, I gathered my coins and emptied the vending machine in the middle-of-the-night hotel corridor with its low electrical hum and its machine for dispensing ice. Hershey bars, cheese crackers, peanut M&Ms. I didn't like the taste of any of that food, it was no more than a means to an end after a long day.

The next day I'd woken early and hungry, with an emptied stomach from the night before. I ate a simple breakfast before the others rose, spread out a map, made phone calls, drove to a remote laboratory, worked calmly and purposefully through the day. We spent the day filming an eminent evolutionary biologist in a laboratory and in a lightless, soundless chamber with a helmet on his head sending weak magnetic waves into the temporal lobes of his brain, in an attempt to stimulate a religious experience. Nothing happened at this supposed climax of our film, months in the making. The director was furious, the biologist disappointed, the cameraman, whose infrared camera lens had broken at the worst possible moment, was keeping out of the firing line. But I was back to being contained, methodical and reliable; nothing was too much for me to handle.

It occurred to me there, for the first time, that I need this behaviour. I no longer know if I am capable without it. I need this side of me to keep the other side going. I can only keep the one going, the strong one, the competent, energetic woman, if the other is allowed to exist too. The threat of disorder, resentment, excess, is all channelled out; it won't come out in public. It's done with, defeated, by the end of the binge. Then the strong, capable person emerges once again.

Telling my family in Uganda just before we left Africa did not alter the path of my illness, as I hoped it would. It has carried on much the same these past few years since we returned to England and I moved to London to work, worsening year upon year, sporadically derailing my days and my weeks and my months, but not quite enough that I cease to function in any visible way. I have to be more careful about hiding it when I visit my parents at their countryside home. It is easy enough to do. It's easy to keep them at arm's length; it always has been, in this respect. I look normal and I appear to behave normally, most of the time. I have a job, I pay my rent, I go out, I have friends, I have a boyfriend, my weight is average. You wouldn't know to look at me, even after all this time.

When, sometimes, they ask me about it, I play it down, or I avoid the question, or I lie. They know it carries on, because I haven't told them it is over, but I have given them the deliberate impression that it's diminished, and that I am working on it, pushing it, easing it, in the right direction. They assume, from what I tell them, that it is under control.

Mum and I turn away from the pond and head slowly, arm in arm again, back down the lane. As we pass the barn I notice, beyond a silvery lichen growing on the rickety wooden fence, that the solid climbing fig against the small red and grey bricks of the barn wall has thickened, stretching out its arms like a crucifix, and up towards the soaring roof. There are no leaves on it yet, but I can see the small bare heads of hundreds of tiny, immature figs.

'Work is good,' I say to Mum. 'In fact, I think I already have my next project lined up. I met a director I really like the other day. I think you'd like her too – she's full of energy. Her name's Fran. When I finish the science film I'm on at the moment I'm going to work with her on a documentary about Alzheimer's, at the BBC again.'

'That does sound interesting,' Mum says.

'Yes, I'm excited about it.'

As we approach the wooden gate at the end of the drive, Mum asks if I know that Wusha ate all the lilies from the pond of an elderly couple who live in a house nearby. I did know. Dad told us that the old lady was so upset that she came round while he was working on the bonfire. She was so angry, he said, that she shook her watering can at him.

I can't imagine that this kind of thing has ever happened to him in his adult life, not since he went to Nigeria to work there during the civil war. At the age of twenty-six he was awarded an MBE for his work during that war, the Biafran war of independence. He once had to preserve the bodies of two doctors, his colleagues and friends, who were dragged out of their hospital in the bush and shot. They were working for the International Red Cross, like Dad. Their bodies were injected with formaldehyde to try to stop them decomposing under the hot sun in the hospital yard, where they had been left when they were shot. When Dad realised they would not be able to get the bodies out, they dug holes in the ground of the nearby churchyard and buried them there. Mum was careful we didn't come home smelling of formaldehyde once we got old enough to dissect dead frogs at school.

'The old lady was very upset indeed about her lilies,' Dad had said, shaking his head, with a slight, mystified smile.

I just can't imagine that he's enjoying these simple, domestic, British interactions. Worse than that, I fear it will reveal some hollowness, some emptiness, to their situation now. And yet.

Mum and I scrape the mud off our boots in the porch of the house, a long bungalow, built by a Nepalese civil servant on his return to England over a hundred years ago. It took them a year to find this home after they came back. As they searched, their map of the south of England, pinned to the wall over the dining table in the old house on the hill by the green, filled with pins and coloured flags. Dad took out a protractor and drew large overlapping circles around gliding clubs, squash courts, tennis courts and golf clubs, around his mother and my aunts and uncles, and they searched roughly in the areas within the circles' radiuses.

They began to hear stories of other Africans returning to England and buying isolated rural properties with something of the wildness of Africa, who realised with time that they could not bear the loneliness; of the friends who spent five years painstakingly restoring a fifteenth-century house on the Yorkshire moors, only to sell up and return to East Africa as soon as they had finished, defeated by the isolation of the bleak moor in winter.

Dad bursts out of the door with a squash racket slung across his back.

'Off to squash,' he says, bending to attach clips to the trouser-ends of his tracksuit. 'I'm cycling in, there's nothing like it on a day like this. Want to come?' he asks.

'No thanks, Dad. I have a few things to do before I go back to London.'

'Can't you stay another night?' he asks.

'No. I'm working tomorrow.'

It's Sunday. A dark Sunday feeling starts growing behind my ribs, a seeding, mossing, spreading, even though I still have a few hours before I have to catch the train.

'I'll be back in an hour or two,' Dad says. 'If you have a chance, do look at the rhododendrons at the back of the house. I've cut everything right back and it's opened up much more light and much more garden. And now you can appreciate their trunks, which really are beautiful things.'

The civil servant, on his return to England from Nepal, brought with him saplings of Nepalese rhododendron which he planted when he built the house. A hundred years later and they have grown into solid trees. Their trunks, hidden from sight, have been exposed by Dad's careful work: beautiful, vigorous trunks, like the intertwining legs of elephants.

Twenty-One

Sussex. Spring 2005

The train curls into the station that evening. London-bound, Platform 2. I watch it coming towards me and feel an unaccustomed peace. I've been making this same journey ever since my parents went to live in the country. Their home has been a constant these past few years, though my own changes habitually. London is such a vast, sprawling city, and I haven't yet found a place within it where I want to stay for longer than six months, or a year at most. So I move often, packing my books and clothes into the back of the car, moving in with friends in flats around the city.

But I decided that I wanted to live alone this time, so I have just begun renting my uncle's basement flat near the river and Battersea Bridge. It is warm and carpeted and lived-in, and I like it there. My uncle has lived there since the sixties, and rents it out whenever he can to go travelling. Across the road from the flat is the soaring red brick of a disused coal-fired power station, its two striking chimneys solid against the changing skies over the river. The chimneys have no purpose now – no longer pouring smoke over London as they did for a hundred years – but they are still beautiful. Perhaps it's something like this, a monument like this, that will make me want to stay in one place for a time, in the city.

The train stops. I choose my door, the one to the carriage nearest me with fewest people in it. There are not many of this type of train still running in the south, I've been told, and it won't be around for long. It isn't something I would usually have noticed, that this is an old model, that it's becoming defunct. It has a rickety, draughty feel to it; to open the door from the inside you have to push down the window and reach for the handle on the outside of the train, but I like that. I clamber in and have to slam the door shut so that the hinge will catch. The carriage shakes.

I sit back and watch the outside slipping past: fields I haven't yet walked in, bridges over unfamiliar country towns, cars stopped in a row by the side of the line. We pause at a station called Christ's Hospital. It must be a beautiful place, with a name like this. I imagine stepping off the train here and walking off into the countryside, the ancient ruins of a hospital rising out of the tufted grass. And perhaps a river with river-dwelling creatures going about their business in the spring sunshine: Ratty and Mole in a low rowing boat, a dragonfly whirring lazily overhead, a willow trailing its branches in the water.

It must be six o'clock in the evening, but the sky is still a light-filled blue; it won't be long before these spring evenings open up into the long full evenings of summer. And today, on the train, unusually, I feel no precarious, unfulfilled expectations of the outside landscape that's slipping past, of wanting to be in it, to be a part of it, to walk in its fields and over its hills and along its rivers.

And now a commuter town where we pause for some minutes; the train connects to another or disconnects, I'm never sure which. From my seat at the window I idly take in the coffee bar on the platform. It is closed. I have no need to summon the thought, it comes to me naturally through years of habit. My mind fills with the image of its offerings when it's open: three-tiered wire trays set either side of the hatch holding brownies, flapjacks, muffins, and sometimes the weighty Dutch biscuits I first discovered from a Dutch friend at boarding school. The ones whose surface is criss-crossed, waffle-like, hiding a dense, chewy middle. I chanced upon them again years later in Oxford, in the covered market, in the delicatessen opposite the butcher.

And then of course, next to the three-tiered trays, there'll be pastries under a glass dome, on a plate, with tongs. Almond croissants and Danish, and others with a sticky white glaze. But not on a Sunday. There is nothing there on a Sunday, and it makes me feel uneasy. Access to food has become my currency. I need it there in an emergency. In London there is always a supplier, day or night, late-opening corner shops or takeaway chicken joints clustered around the tube and train stations.

We slide out of the station. I slip a piece of paper out of my bag and unfold it on my lap. It is a year-to-a-view calendar, printed on a single side of paper, that I fold into four and carry with me wherever I go. I started doing it when we returned to England, drawing a red circle, fine-nibbed, around every day that I lost control. I was trying to see patterns, trying to track what was happening in the hope of finding some link between periods and binges, between weekdays and weekends, between summer and winter. I never managed to identify any patterns, but the habit stayed. It has become my simple method of keeping track of how often I binge.

Three clear days in a row, not bad. If I can get through today then it will be four. Last month, February, I had a full clear week. I stare blankly at February. I can't think where that clear week came from, what it was about that week that made it a clear week, what the quality of my thinking was that was different, and how I can go back to that. The first three months of the calendar are covered with neat red circles, scattered liberally and with no apparent logic to them. It was the same for the whole of last year, and the same the year before that.

I wonder if someone else would be able to see any pattern in this, would be able to make the connections that I fail to make. I don't know. Sometimes I think about looking for professional help again, but I can't see how a third party can help with this. I told my family, and for a time I hoped that that would alter its course, but I have engineered it so that they are excluded, so that they can't help even though they want to. It just isn't something I can share, or talk about. That's just the way it is: it has no logic. It comes from nowhere. It makes no sense. If it makes no sense to me I don't know how I could make it make sense to somebody else.

I fold up the calendar and look out of the window again. Perhaps the truth is that I shall never be capable of controlling this, I am stuck on this track and I can't get off. And even a professional would make no headway. That would close down my last option, so I avoid it.

We're in the London suburbs now: playing-fields, rows of Victorian terraced houses backing on to green space. We'll be at Clapham Junction in fifteen minutes. If I'm going to see Alex tonight, I'll have to arrange it now. He lives in South London. Alex and I have been together, off and on, for a few years now. We were friends at Oxford, and began seeing each other in our final year, then we met up again when I returned from Uganda. It has never been a straightforward or easy relationship, but we keep coming back to each other, we know each other so well now. We fight all the time. Alex is a fighter. He is a much better fighter than I am, because although I happily fight back, I tend to take it personally and so it lingers far longer than it should.

Alex comes from a family of fighters. If they are angry, they fight. They fight across the kitchen table of the family home, they fight in the car on the way to the cinema, they fight over the phone to their father who lives in an African capital city, investing in jungle ventures and trying to cajole the government into paying him for the Land Rovers he sold them, but which they haven't yet paid for. Their father still lives in the house where Alex and his sister grew up, two tall, blond kids riding horses and speaking a fast African French. There is a strange kind of honesty in the family's belligerence. And so Alex fights with me too – he doesn't think there is anything unusual about that. Being with Alex means I am not alone, there is always somewhere I can go: left on Lavender Hill, cut through the urban playground with its pigeons and drunks, left again down the hill. It means my life in London is full, busy. I balk at the uncontainedness of solitude, and the simple unpredictability of being in my own company.

I've told Alex about what I do. He has known for a long time, but it has just become part of our fabric. I keep it hidden, and everything carries on. Perhaps there isn't that much wrong with me, or that much different about me. Maybe we all have our downtime, our need to privately break down, and we channel it in different ways. If only my way was less destructive.

I dial his number, reluctant to pull away from the somnolent journey.

'Hello,' he says. He says it quickly, there is nothing languid in the way he talks, even when he isn't high. Still, I'm happy to hear his voice. I picture him in his front room, long legs propped up on the table, computer on his lap, his thoughts exploding in twenty different directions simultaneously.

'Did you have a good weekend at your folks'?'

'Yes, thanks,' I say.

He's not interested in the detail. He's wired, I can tell from his voice.

'And you, did you have a good weekend?' I ask. He doesn't need to tell me about it, I know what pattern it will have followed. He won't have slept since yesterday.

'Not bad,' he says. 'Stayed up working on a spreadsheet most of last night. Dan is here. He's asleep on the sofa.'

Dan is Alex's housemate. His weekends are usually benders. He's out all night at clubs, then he drinks and smokes in front of the football with the curtains half-drawn against the daylight. To make up for it he spends every night of the week at the gym; he talks quietly and seldom, blends fruit drinks and goes to bed early to get up early for his job as a trader in the City, dressed in immaculate suits, full of promises about cleaning up. But he can't resist the weekend indulgences.

Alex's is more of a constant indulgence: he doesn't swing from one extreme to another and he still manages to work hard, maybe even harder, even with the drug-taking; it only seems to heighten his natural hyperactivity. Even with the football on he'll have his laptop open on his lap, working on a business model, tweaking spreadsheets, cracking the knuckles of his long fingers.

And only rarely, during comedowns at dawn, while I try to sleep on the other side of the bed, has he ever expressed any desire to change the way things are.

'Shall I come over? Or . . .' I let it go so he can fill in.

'Up to you,' he says. 'Maybe not a great idea. Football's on later. And I should get some sleep before Monday morning.'

'You don't want to go out for something to eat?' I know what the answer is; I'm not sure why I ask, just to make a point, that this is what we had planned.

'No, not really,' he says, and I can hear the slightest trace of remorse in his voice.

His doorbell rings.

'That's Seb,' he says.

Seb is Alex's dealer.

We've seen little of one another lately. Other than working, he has weekends like these, blinds half-closed on the day, daylit ashtrays. And a screen of footballers running up and down a pitch, doing it over and over again in a seemingly eternal loop.

Still, I find myself there sometimes, making it my world too. But not so much lately because I've started seeing someone else. So I don't really mind that Alex is so caught up in his own thing, that he never seems to stop; in fact it helps with the deception, and the guilt. And for his part he is relieved that I'm not interrupting things for him and fighting with him. It makes a change.

Damian is different. There are no curtains on his windows. His apartment is open to the light that floods in to the top of the building where he lives in King's Cross, high above Pentonville Road. Pentonville Road: light blue on the Monopoly board, along with Euston Road and Angel Islington. Real places, it turns out.

But Damian's habit is even more copious than Alex's. At least Damian's is recreational. He doesn't stay in with the telly on and the day outside. He's out working and running around and taking risks and having adventures; he's arrested and falls into holes and smashes all his teeth, he takes photographs of caged bears in Ukraine and has a mistress in Zambia, and he comes back to a minimalist flat with a view of St Paul's lit up on the London skyline, a series of paintings of nudes against exposed brick, and a kitchen drawer where he keeps his cocaine and his rolling papers. He likes to smoke it, it's more of a hit that way.

I wonder if Alex wonders why I'm not fighting, why I'm not spending as much time with him, why I don't need him as much as I usually do. The only thing that absorbs him lately is his work and his nights like these. He probably hasn't even noticed.

As the train pulls into London Victoria, my phone rings. It's Anna. I don't answer it. I don't feel like being accountable to my sister; I don't feel like pretending that everything is normal. She lives with her boyfriend now, and works in a job she moderately likes. She cycles on London's commons and plays squash at a club, and cooks and goes dancing with her friends. She has always known how to do normal things well. We don't see one another much in London.

I find straightforward conversation, with the people who know me well, difficult and often empty, so I avoid it much of the time. I'm fine at work, I'm fine with Damian or in Alex's frenetic world, I'm fine when I'm out at parties, it's just the normal bits of life that confound me. I can't see how anyone can have a normal conversation, can watch television, can find their way through an open-ended space of time, without being dogged by the idea of doing something else, something full-blooded, to pin it all down.

My phone vibrates. It's a message from Damian, wanting to know if I am coming up to see him tonight.

The other passengers are in the aisles, pulling bags down from the overhead rack, pulling on coats. They stream past the windows heading for the barriers at Victoria. But I stay still for a moment and look at my hands, thinking about my options. I am the last on the train. I don't mind that. I don't mind being the last through the barriers either, avoiding the swell of bodies and their purposefulness; I prefer leaving slowly, in the wake, where it is still.

I'll go and see Damian. I know it isn't the sensible choice, but I want to see him. I'd like to be there in his high-up apartment full of light, where you can see what kind of day it is, laughing at stories of adventures and mishaps, watching the city's sky change colour from evening to night to morning. I know that I should go home, go back to my flat and organise myself for the week of work ahead. But I'd be alone that way, and the chances are remote of following through on what I set out to do, on the ordinary stuff of daily life: the cleaning, and the cobweb on the window in the little kitchen; the simple act of sitting down to watch a programme, of preparing a meal and eating it, safely, with composure. I know how seldom I ever manage to follow through on simple tasks like these, the simple preparing of the ground that others do so much better, so that good things rise unfurling through rich soil.

Twenty-Two

Cambridge. Early summer, 2005

Two months later I'm in a café in Cambridge, waiting to meet a mother and daughter who I hope might be the family I've been looking for, for the Alzheimer's documentary I've begun researching with Fran. I've enjoyed the rhythm of the last couple of months, of cycling to work every morning in West London, up crowded main roads and across residential backstreets, the cherry trees of Olympia in blossom as spring eased itself slowly towards summer. At the main White City offices I lock my bike to the bike rack, and enter the building under the weighty letters of the corporation's name. The letters make me think of the World Service pips, or the strange dissonant trumpet that heralds *Focus on Africa* playing on the shortwave radio on the table at the lake in Ethiopia, or on the car radio when our parents would tune in on the hour to listen to the news as we children yawned and complained on the back seat.

'Aren't you interested in what's going on in the world?' Dad would ask, and we would roll our eyes at each other.

The mornings are good. The mornings are when I feel hopeful, optimistic about my day, when I am at my strongest; a new day, a clean slate, I am full of determination and resolve and lightness. It is as the day wears on that my defences grow thinner, when things might go awry.

I order olives, bread and red wine while I wait in the café. Soon Christine and Fiona, the mother and daughter, will arrive. I watch as the café fills, as the patrons stop their bikes against lamp posts in the clear light of the street outside. I watch them all, the academics and the students, a pair of women with frizzy greying hair and large rings who take the table next to mine.

The bread arrives in a basket, soft focaccia, with an outer crunch and a shine of oil and herbs. I tear pieces off and dip them into the oil pooling around the olives. I'll make sure I eat a proper meal when the women arrive. Drinking wine, especially in the daytime, always lowers my defences against the bingeing impulse later on. If I eat I can at least take hunger out of the equation.

I open my notebook, and glance again through my notes. Christine's neurologist, at Addenbrooke's Hospital in Cambridge, told me that although her early-onset dementia appeared to be advancing relatively rapidly in some areas, her facility with language and her ability to articulate were not being eroded at the same pace as her memory. She had spent so many years, he said, exercising the language part of her brain in her capacity as editor at Cambridge University Press that it was more resistant to the encroaching dementia.

Light splashes against the street-facing windows. They're late, but I'm happy to wait in this in-between time. These moments have seemed so rare, lately, these moments of equilibrium. But while I wait, contained by the prospect of their arrival, I can let down my guard. The wine arrives with three glasses. I pour myself a glass, sit back, watch the café's edges soften and the windows gradually mist up, and I begin to eavesdrop on the conversation of the women with the large rings and the loud voices. I'd like to close my eyes, lay my head on the table, sleep. For months now I feel I have dipped in and out of a current of tiredness that I can't seem to shift. As soon as I stop moving, it comes back. On the tube, on trains and buses, I rest my head against anything I can find: the glass partition, the door, the bus window, and fall abruptly into a deep, unconscious kind of sleep.

I check my watch. Twenty minutes late. I'll call Fiona. I know she hasn't forgotten. I called her from the train on the way down to confirm the time and place, to tell her I'm wearing a red scarf so she knows who I am. I pick up my phone and as I scroll down to find her number, Fiona appears beside me and tells me she can't find her mother. We will have to look for her.

We search the streets between the café and Christine's home, but there's no sign. Eventually we reach the street where Christine lives. It is a narrow one-way street of terraced Cambridge houses. It's just the kind of place I might have imagined her living, with rusted bikes tied to lamp posts, an air of gentle bookishness, of down-at-heel scholarliness about it, the kind of place I could imagine myself living, in another life. Fiona knocks and Christine answers the door, looking surprised.

'Weren't we supposed to be meeting in that café?' she asks. 'I waited there for a good half-hour.'

'You and I were meeting at mine, Mum, and then both of us were going together to the café to meet Caroline. I wrote it on the wall.' Fiona points to a yellow note curling away from the wall by the door.

Christine ushers me in. The room is cluttered with books and papers and notebooks, hand-written memos and photographs paper its walls. Beyond this room and down a step is a narrow kitchen lying alongside a garden, where I can just make out, beyond the broad, veined leaves of a vine filtering light through the window, a small, haphazard English garden.

She sweeps a pile of old newspapers from an armchair and beckons for me to sit, then perches at her writing table, balancing a glass of wine on her open diary. The diary is filled with spidery, energetic writing and a chaos of asterisks, arrows and underlinings. Fiona leans against the kitchen door into the garden, smoking, looking out more than in.

Christine and I talk. This is my chance to get the measure of them and their situation, to see whether Fran and I might be able to make a film with them and about them. Christine explains the notes on the walls, stuck with pins and Sellotape, reminders of things both small and big. She writes these notes on the walls, Christine tells me, so that she doesn't forget. The name of the prime minister, the price of the *Guardian*, the names of the three men she married and her date of birth sixty-five years ago.

She points at a picture of a lighthouse stuck on the wall above the cooker.

'Southwold,' Christine calls over her shoulder to Fiona. 'Do you remember our holidays in Southwold, darling?'

'I do, Mum.' A drift of cigarette smoke floats up to the leaves of the garden's cherry tree.

'I love the sea,' Christine tells me. 'There's nowhere I'm

happier. I'd love to just start swimming and not come back, one day. That's how I'd like to go.' She fingers the corner of a journal, thoughtfully. 'I don't mind my Alzheimer's really,' she says. 'In fact I'd probably be a bit lost without it now. But I know it goes in only one direction.'

Behind her Fiona is looking up at the clouded evening sky, at the roses scrambling over the garden wall.

'I'd rather the sea than end up in a home,' Christine persists. Then she shrugs and picks up a slim volume open on the table next to her diary.

'Joan Didion,' she says with nostalgia. '*Slouching Towards Bethlehem.*' She savours the words of the title. 'Have you read it?' she asks. I tell her I haven't.

'Take my copy,' she says. She thrusts the book into my hands. 'I can't read it anyway.' She shakes her head. 'Give it back to me when you've finished, if you like. All this is Fiona's when I die so I suppose I ought not to give it all away.'

'Oh, Mother,' Fiona says. She pulls the kitchen door closed so that we are cut off from the garden. 'Stop talking about dying.'

I order a minicab to take me back to the station. When it arrives I take Christine's book with me because I know I'll be coming back. I am certain that Fran will want these two as the participants in our film and I would happily spend the coming summer months and the autumn in their company, if they will agree to it.

As the taxi crawls towards the station in thick traffic along Parker's Piece, I start to dip back into my exhaustion. I rest my head against the window and let my thoughts wander. I have a dull journey ahead of me, back down to King's Cross, then across London on the tube, then a second tube, then twenty minutes on foot to my front door. But it's all right, because I've already decided that I can fill the journey with food. I allow the impulse to come to me, doors wide open.

I saw the chocolate-covered marshmallow teacakes on my way in through the station earlier in the afternoon. Sixteen of them, individually wrapped. Unwrap, eat, drop the foil into the plastic bag, reach for the next one casually, as though I were an ordinary person eating biscuits on the train. One after another after another. I saw cakes too. Cakes are harder. I can sink my fingers into their soft belly, pull out chunks, but it's messy, open to suspicion, fingernails brown with chocolate, shirt front messed with crumbs, and it's hard to control the size of the piece. I end up shoving it in fast, anxious I might get noticed, caught. And that anxiety spoils the moment, the moment of it entering my mouth, the soft melting against the inside of my cheeks.

My mouth is watering now, my tiredness pushed aside. Now I can't wait to get to the shop at the station. Soon my journey will be filled to the edges, replete, stuffed brimful with food. I'll text Damian from the train and tell him that I can't see him tonight, that I'm working late in Cambridge. I reassure myself that I'll finish most of the binge before I reach home, that way it's just the last throes, the finishing off, that'll need doing, and that way I'll still get some sleep tonight. But I know how it always drags on. Whole hours disappear, but I resolve not to let that happen, not this time.

We ease out of the jam and into a flow of cars up the side of the green. I check the time again: eight minutes until the train leaves. I feel the tension up the side of my neck.

'Can I pay you now and get a receipt, please? I'm in a bit of a hurry.'

I place a ten-pound note into the hand he holds out next to the head-rest. He tears off a blank receipt, hands it back to me with the change.

'You'll be fine,' he says. 'I'll get you there for the King's Cross train.'

He pulls into the station, curves around to the front. I jump out and run through the entrance. I have my train ticket in my hand. To my left the open doors of the shop, the rows of marshmallow teacakes and queues at the tills, in front of me the boards that show only three minutes before the train leaves on Platform 5A. I can't do it. For a desperate second I think about stealing the biscuits, the marshmallow teacakes, but there's a security guard at the entrance in a uniform too tight for him. He is staring into the concourse, blankly.

Two minutes to go. I can't do it. I cross the barriers, run to the end of the platform, past the kiosk, past a chocolate dispenser with its Twirls and Wispas. I scrabble in my pocket for some change for the chocolate machine but drop a handful onto the platform. The coins scatter as the whistle blows. I run for the train doors, leap onto the train just as the doors slide closed.

Cambridge Station glides away, Cambridge University Press, where Christine was an editor, and then countryside. I have failed. I have no choice now but to accept this bitter disappointment.

I am shaking. Order, I need order. I take off my jacket and lay it on the seats opposite, I clear an empty crisp packet and a bottle top from my table into the bin by the doors. I wipe crumbs and a tea stain off the table, then lay out the contents of my bag. I slip my work notebook back into my bag, binding on top. I return my phone and pen to the side pocket. The O in DEFOE, organisation. If I can control this environment, clear it out, it will seep into my brain and still it.

I shake out my shawl, fold it in half, then in half again, then roll it up and place it at the top of the bag. I pull the taxi receipt out of my pocket and fill it in carefully – the date, the amount paid, where I was going and for which project – then put it in my wallet and replace my wallet in the bag. Then I sit back, hold the book Christine gave me in my hands, and stare out of the window as the train journeys south. I sit still, watching the darkness slide past the windows. Silence.

No matter what I do, I can't reach food. I think back to what I have eaten in the day. The bread and olives are OK. I had a stuffed baked potato at lunchtime. All safe foods. Two glasses of wine. I haven't crossed the line, not yet. I can still stay this side of it. There is still the possibility of a peaceful evening ahead, the possibility of safety. The waves that were crashing in my head slow and still.

I open Joan Didion. My hands are no longer shaking. '*Slouching Towards Bethlehem* was the first time I had dealt directly and flatly with the evidence of atomization, the proof that things fall apart.' I look up again, out of the window, and think about Christine. I think of her struggling to read these words, as if she needed proof now that things fall apart. I picture her brain with a healthy bulge in the language lobe, like an escaping inner tube, free from the plaques and tangles scattered like spidery limescale across the rest of the failing muscle.

Still, the ending is the same for all of us. Things fall apart, there is nothing anyone can do about it.

Twenty-Three

Southwold, Suffolk.
Late summer, 2005

It was only five months ago that Christine said she'd like to get into the sea at Southwold and keep swimming, but things have moved on rapidly since then.

Fran and I have travelled back and forth between London and Cambridge, as the spring turned to summer and the summer began to wane, chronicling the changes in her and her daughter's lives. I watch Christine sometimes and know that she's trying to remember why we're here at all, why we're interested in her. I've also noticed that she's become adept at covering mistakes she makes in conversation. She's at an awkward stage in her dementia, still aware of the changes and the mistakes she is making, and conscious of the gaps that are appearing in her memory.

She has forgotten that she would like to disappear in the sea at Southwold, so we have brought her here to swim at the fading end of the summer. I'm in my bikini wading into the cold water.

I pull my hairband out of my hair to stop my hair knotting around it in the water and slip it onto my wrist. My hair falls loosely down my back and I feel it brush against the curve of my lower back. I haven't had it cut for months and months. I like it this way, long and wild.

I press down on the ornate horseshoe-shaped ring between my breasts that holds together the two top triangles of material, striped an earthy red and brown and gold. On a smaller-breasted woman this horseshoe ring is supposed to lie flat against the middle of the chest, but on me it is suspended between my breasts, taut, pulled in both directions, and looks as though it might give. I can see a green seam of rust running up one side of the curve. I have worn this bikini through a few summers now.

As soon as the water is up to my thighs I'll dive in. I know that after the initial shock I am flooded with a sense of clarity and aliveness as the water pulls against my skin, in every little space and on every plane the cold, salty sea: in the corners of my eyes, inside my thighs, between my toes, along my ribs; my hair pulls backwards instantly through the water, a cold sting against my scalp, and I am alive.

Just before I dive in I look back to shore and see Christine and Fiona appear at the top of the steps leading down to the beach. The cameraman and Fran are standing halfway up the beach. Fran is in her swimming costume too. The cameraman has his lens pointed out to sea, towards me. I dive in.

I'll swim far enough out to sea so that I'm not visible in shot and then I'll tread water, just in case Christine gets confused about the direction of the beach, or the cold water jogs her memory.

Fran wades into the water and dives, swims out towards me with strong strokes. She and I have made a good partnership in this film, and I have been impressed by her instinct for teasing out the larger preoccupation from the jumble of events and ordinary happenings in Christine and Fiona's lives, by her instinct for a coherent story in what we have followed over the past six months, as Christine has struggled against her predicament.

Fran swims out until she is parallel with me, with about twenty yards' distance between us, then she waves to me and to the cameraman on the beach.

Christine and Fiona come down to the water's edge. Christine unwraps her towel from her shoulders and hands it to her daughter, then strides towards the waves. She is not a beautiful woman but she is elegant and flirtatious and bold. Men have always been part of her scene. They have come and gone. She is wearing an all-in-one bathing suit above long legs. She wades in unflinching, then lowers herself in gently and breast-strokes out to sea, her chin tilted up, her long hair trailing in the water behind her. I swim a little further out. She rolls onto her back and tips her head back into the water. Her knees rise and fall as she floats out, she makes circles under the water with her arms. I see that she is smiling up at the sky. She is free, I can see it on her face, just her and the swells of the sea.

She is not going any further, now swimming in contented circles not too far from shore. I don't need to watch her now. I dive under then break the surface, and again, and again, each time swimming down deeper. I imagine the blood pushing through all my capillaries and veins and arteries, I feel myself tautening, tightening, against the cold, shrinking in against muscle and sinew, my body lengthening as I stretch down into the grey depths. Up again, and now Christine is heading to shore. She staggers in the waves that break around her ankles, and Fiona comes to her, the towel held out to her. Christine pulls it around her shoulders and they walk back up the beach, together, away from the sea.

I know this will be the end of our story. We will leave her happy, swimming in the sea, coming fleetingly back to herself, in the final scene, and Fran and I will move on to something else. We have one more day at Southwold, then we will return to London and Christine and Fiona will go back to Cambridge and carry on with their lives. I have a sense of foreboding about going back to my life in London. I need something like this, like this sea, to remind me that I am still vigorous, capable of feeling this kind of aliveness.

I won't stop at King's Cross this time, on my way back into the city. I don't any more. Damian is in Zambia again. He rented out his flat so he could save money to pay for the work to fix the teeth he broke months ago, on a previous visit to Zambia, when he fell into a ditch and smashed his jaw. It was late at night, he said, there was no electricity, he was walking home and he fell into an open hole left by men working on the road. It's the kind of thing that happens to Damian, and we laughed about it when he told me the story, his black eyes glittering, smiling through his broken teeth. He hadn't fixed them yet, because since he left his job at the paper where he worked, his freelance ventures haven't been as plentiful or as lucrative as he hoped, and money is tight.

By the time he decided on this plan to go back to Zambia we

had already started arguing. I had promised to break it off with Alex early in the summer, and hadn't, so it followed that things began to disintegrate. We started fighting about small things. Pointless, vitriolic fights, like why he never stubbed out his cigarettes, but left them to burn themselves out slowly, a wisp of grey-brown smoke trailing steadily, uselessly, up to the ceiling until they quietly died at the filter. I could see his circumspection growing. Arguing about small things was not part of his plan, nor mine.

He is in Zambia and we have decided not to see one another when he returns. I'll miss the adventure, and the feeling of an opening-up of possibilities when I was with him, even if it wasn't real. I'll miss the view of St Paul's on the London skyline. At night it is lit, in soft angled beams, and still it is solid, unmoving, constant. I know St Paul's, I know what it looks like, I could point it out to a stranger to the city, and that makes me from here.

Before long I will have to pluck up the courage to come clean with Alex and end that relationship, too, in a final way. I am tired of worrying about it, and tired of thinking about it, and I know that it isn't right but I haven't convinced myself yet. I'm sure we have both known for a long time, probably since the beginning, that if it is this difficult, then it can't work. But the thought of it actually ending, the prospect of the absence of the relationship, of more time in my own company, struggling to maintain what is increasingly a near-impossible private equilibrium, scares me off from dealing with it.

The sea is turning an evening grey and I am starting to shiver. Fran has swum back, but I don't want to follow her out, not yet. I stay out at sea until I see the cameraman lift the camera off the tripod and the sound recordist take off his head-phones. I watch them both walk away from me along the sand, then I swim quickly back to shore.

Twenty-Four

London. Winter, 2005

Back in London things unravel quickly as winter deepens. Lifeless branches of trees reach up into a silver-cold, empty sky. The weekends are the time I dread the most. I try to fill them, to keep busy with friends and going out and seeing Alex, but there is still time to fill, empty hours and between hours, to fill with food. I spend time by the river near my flat, walking, or running, looking for corners of the riverside I don't know, but I can't escape the bareness of the trees, reaching towards nothing. I know I have to keep on, I have no choice.

I arrange one Saturday morning to meet Hugh for tea, and later that day I walk briskly towards the café to rid myself of the staleness from the days before. Crowds flow around me as I emerge onto Oxford Street into a sea of black winter coats. I swing my arms as I walk, willing a fresh, oxygenated blood to clear out the cobwebs in my head. But when I arrive and settle in opposite Hugh, all I can see beyond the collar of his shirt are the rows of Italian breads and cakes in the corner of things, calling my attention, and the slice of carrot cake on my plate is so small and insubstantial, so fleeting, it will be gone too quickly and leave me wanting more. I promise myself food afterwards, and in the momentary glow of the prospect I am able to relax enough to concentrate on our conversation, to muster an enthusiasm I don't feel, to suppress the feeling that all I want is to be somewhere else. I visit the supermarket on the way home, cut through the council estate, try not to catch any reflection of myself as I hurry home with my bag of shopping.

The start of the working week is a relief. Every morning I carry my bike up the stairs from the basement flat, then cycle in the heavy morning traffic up the North End Road to work. London has won the Olympic bid and it looks as though Fran and I might work together on a series of documentaries about the build-up to the Games. In the meantime I'm writing pitches for other films we might make. I buy myself a coffee when I arrive at work, and chat with my colleagues, who I like. I'll sometimes have a hot breakfast in the canteen with Harish before the day begins, if it isn't his shift on the turnstiles at the entrance to the building. I like his easy chatter and his humour, and his disconnectedness from anything in my world. He leans forward on the canteen chair and tells me about his family and the house he lives in, and his dream of leaving work and trying a different line of business.

The breakfast fills me up enough so that hunger pangs aren't distracting me and derailing my concentration. In my lunch hour, if I am not eating with colleagues in the canteen or at an outside restaurant, I'll order up old documentary films from the BBC archives, and watch them, leaning against the windows in my corner of the open-plan office, headphones on, rain trickling down the outside of the panes, eating a sandwich; contained by the wall at my back and the headphones on my ears, and the warm hum of the still building. The editor tells me that my contract will be renewed and I negotiate a pay rise with the production manager.

On my way home I stop at the curry house, halfway down the North End Road. I veer onto the pavement, leave my bike against a lamp post, unlocked, and order the meal special, a foil tray full of rice and the day's curry from under the glass counter for £4.75. The Pakistani server fills it generously, patting it down with the back of the spoon. As he snaps on the plastic lid a film of curry sauce spreads across its underbelly. I cycle home as quickly as I can, the curry in a plastic bag in my rucksack warming my back where it touches. If I cycle fast it will still be hot when I get home. I'll tip it onto a plate and eat it with a spoon. It will give me enough energy to then walk to the shop for more supplies. And that's what I do.

Finished. I wash my face. I look in the mirror and I'm shocked that the face looking back at me is not the same face I had before and during the binge, the heavy, ugly face. These eyes are still alive, there is even something beautiful in this face, and I am so surprised by my reflection that I stand still and watch my face, my real eyes, mouth, nose and cheekbones, which seem so unfamiliar to me now.

'Alex, it's me,' I say. 'I'd like to come over. We need to talk.'

He says it isn't a good time, can't we talk tomorrow? I say no, it has to be now. He says no, can't it wait? And I know he knows what I am going to say. He has known it's been coming for a long time. And so I tell him there and then, on the phone, that the relationship is over, and I tell him about the affair. I tell him so that he will decide for himself, and see for himself, that there is no going back.

I know his eyes will have gone a blank red. It's what happens when he gets into a rage. His eyes change colour from blue to red, and he has no control over what he says. He wants to know who it is.

'His name was Damian. You don't know him. And anyway . . .'

'I don't give a fuck about Damian!' he shouts.

Later that night he comes to the flat, he shouts some more and then he leaves, slamming the door as hard as he can, shouting into the empty middle-of-the-night street by the river. I hear the revving of his car's engine. I picture him accelerating down the Embankment, past the Albert Bridge, past the statue of the boy flying over the back of a dolphin, holding on to its fin. He looks just like that boy, just the same – he has the same arched feet, the same hands, the boy's leanness and long torso, but all grown beyond an average size to a point just beyond his own control.

Twenty-Five

London. Midwinter, 2005

It is two weeks after I split up with Alex that I miss the bus. I have been at a party and am standing at the bus stop in the rain, in the middle of the night. The number 10 has just pulled away from me, but still I shout after it. And then something finally gives, the worn-thin fabric inside that is the difference between carrying on and not carrying on, and I find myself there on the pavement, taken aback by the screaming, my screaming. Faces stare out at me from the bus as it retreats, unsteady faces through rain and blinking brake lights. I run into the traffic and stop a black taxi, huddle in the corner on its clean, shining seat against the far window. It's then, as we pull out into the traffic, all muffled sounds, red lights and rain streaming down the windows, that I hear a little disembodied voice, my sister's, coming from my bag, calling out to me. I fumble for the phone, hang up as quickly as I can, but she calls me straight back and I have to answer it. I know I have to. I tell her I am safe. I tell her I will call her in the morning. The black cab pulls up outside my door, outside the Victorian railings and the chimneys stretching up into the dark night.

'You'll be all right,' the driver says to me, and I am surprised to see his face looking back at me through the partition.

I close the front door, drop my bag onto the carpet, pull my clothes off and leave them in a pile where they fall. I climb into bed and cover my face with the pillow.

Watery faces worry at the margins of my sleep, and when I wake the following morning I lie still and ignore the light coming round the sides of the heavy curtains. No, I do not need to keep on. If I lie still enough it is as though I do not exist, so I lie as still as I can. It is easier than fighting my way through another day.

If I lie still enough and still my brain, if I breathe little and stay here, I will not feel it crashing in on me. Breathe, in out, in out, slowly. But there it is spreading up through my stomach, around the chambers of my heart, overwhelming me, overcoming me, an unavoidable consciousness of being, of being not enough, of being too much. Help, I say, in my head, into the pale dawn light, and then I pause, waiting to hear a voice, something, anything, come back to me. I say it again, trying not to jog the space around me. Nothing.

Life slips away, runs away, water over boulders, over the backs of the wildebeest, and leaves me here without it.

I know I can no longer carry on, not like this. I see this more clearly than I have ever seen it. But while there is still light coming around the curtains I know that I am alive and that I have no choice but to press on. *Get up*, I think. One foot in front of the other. Get up, keep moving. I know that there has to be a next step, another day. But still I don't move. I can't.

I give up. There is a blue sky, across the road, above the soaring chimneys of the power station, but it is not for me.

Anna heard me shouting. And because she did it means it is real and it happened. I can't bury it and pretend it never did; I can't consign it, like so much else, to the dimension other people don't see. I have been exposed. My sister will be worried, she will be waiting, this morning, for my call. She will have called my parents too and they will be worried. They will be waiting; they will want to know what is happening, what has happened. I am accountable. It is a small seed, but I can't dislodge it, this accountability.

The phone is in my hand. I hear the ringtone, the phone ringing out into the corners of their country garden, glancing over the wheelbarrow, over the logs, splitting and spreading at the tall trees, bouncing back, multiplying until my head is filled with a shrill, insistent noise. My mother answers and the noise cuts dead.

'It's me, Mum,' I say.

In the background I hear my father's voice. They are both talking to me.

'I can come and get her right now,' Dad is saying. 'I can be there in no more than a couple of hours.'

'He's right,' Mum says. 'Just come home. Here, speak to your Dad too,' and she hands over the phone.

'Let us come and get you,' he says. 'Come home.'

Mum takes the phone back and keeps talking, soothing, asking me what's happening, what has happened. I want to put my head on her chest, and stop.

* * *

Dad backs the car out of the drive, turns left through the tunnel of overhanging trees in the lane that leads past the barn. There is no antenna swinging wide. He doesn't need the antenna here.

I sit with an overnight bag on my lap. I have put a toothbrush into it, but I can't think what else I will need. I call Anna; I have to. I tell her what happened. I tell her Dad is coming to collect me.

'We need to do something about this,' she says. 'It has gone on for too long. I just know we can think of something. I'll come as soon as I can.' I hear her exhale. I see her mouth, set, soft, serious; her eyes brown and thinking.

I sit under the skylight in the living room, waiting, sitting quite still so I don't set in motion another sequence of wrong events. I think of my father coming to get me, moving steadily up the A24, dots appearing on a map of Great Britain on the wall of his study, marking his route. Dad knows his way anywhere, I wish I had that skill. He can find his way to anywhere in East Africa, identify any lake, any river, any escarpment, any forest or jungle or desert landscape or irrigation scheme from the air, high Cessna wings tilting this way and that, to give him a good view of the earth below.

'Pop 75000' was written on one of the maps in the office in Addis. Arrows spilled out to it and from it, and I'd asked him what it meant.

'It means there are seventy-five thousand refugees currently living in that refugee camp. That is only a very rough estimate. Some of the refugees in the camp have more than one ID so they can collect more than one allocation of rations. And many of them aren't actually refugees at all – they are people from the local area, which is a very poor desert region, who see what is being handed out in the camps and decide to join them for a time. The arrows show the movement of food and where it comes from' – he pointed at the map and followed the arrow northwards – 'some coming up from Addis, cargo ships coming in to Djibouti and overland from there. It isn't the most direct route, but with the fighting between here and Eritrea we can no longer bring it in through Asmara. You remember Asmara, we drove there last summer.' He pointed at the Eritrean port on the Red Sea. I do remember that journey. I remember the colonial Italian port, I remember a bell tower rising out of the palm trees.

One foot in front of the other foot in front of the other foot. I step over the clothes still in the hallway where I left them in a pile the night before. I remember the door key. We don't talk much in the car on the way back to my parents' house. We don't need to. Dad is here to help, and that is all. It is said. I have failed, and DEFOE has failed, and I don't need to pretend any longer. I know for certain, and for the first time, that I cannot do this by myself. That every turn and every step I have taken has led me into a brick wall.

I sit still, hunched, watching out of the window, staying as still as I can so that I don't trigger the wrong series of things again. Dad reaches over and grips my shoulder.

Twenty-Six

The following morning, at my parents' home in Sussex.
Winter, 2005

William sits next to me on the bed. Our arms are touching, the fine hairs on our forearms rub against each other. We sit facing the closed curtains. My brother is on his way to southern Ethiopia, to guide a travel writer and journalist down a remote stretch of the Omo River, which flows into Lake Turkana in northern Kenya, but he has come to our parents' home to see us before he leaves. I wonder if Mum called him yesterday to ask him to come. I don't want to open the curtains, even though I don't want him to see me like this, keeping out the day. I look down at my hands.

'I'm just . . .' I can't think what to say to him, how I can possibly explain. 'I'm just depressed,' I say. I settle on this thought; it's an easy one, it seems to cover quite a lot.

William rarely sees me like this, our lives don't overlap enough for this kind of intimacy, and besides, I keep these feelings of darkness private, as much as I can. It has been years since I told them about my problem in Uganda, and years since my father came up with the magic formula, 'Be Positive to DEFOE', and now, sitting here next to my brother, facing the curtains, unable to explain, I see how little progress I have made. I rub one foot on top of the other and hold my breath. If I hold my breath I can trap it in there, the panic that keeps welling up underneath the paralysis. If I focus on the particular ball of tightness in the spot where I imagine my ribs join, in the middle of my chest, then at least I can keep my eyes trained on the enemy. I don't want to cry.

The house is winter quiet, a muffled sound of wind and leaves outside, a tick as the radiator contracts.

'Maybe you could think of it like the migration of the wildebeest,' William says.

I take my eyes away from my hands in my lap and focus instead on the familiar birthmark he has on the inside of his forearm.

'It's seasonal,' he explains, 'it's a natural rhythm in nature. The wildebeest migrate every year. It just happens, it's part of life's cycle, the ebbs and flows of life.'

The idea of herds of migrating wildebeest crossing the Serengeti, plunging into rivers, braving crocodiles and lions to get to the new grass after the rains comforts me. I remember them on their endless trek; pitiful, ugly creatures, heads bowed. We flew overhead in Dad's Piper, our shadow skipping over their hunched backs, and left them far behind.

'Hmm. Yes,' I say. I'm not sure what he means. The birthmark on his arm looks like a brown puddle full of miniature tadpoles.

'What I mean is that perhaps if we accept these things, that life is a seasonal ebb and flow, perhaps it would be easier,' he says. 'Accepting the lows might make it easier to bear them.'

He's right. This black, bleak, soulless nothingness is like a welling wave. It comes and it goes; it ebbs and flows. It always dissipates in the end. It always has done. I have always managed to come back. I am grateful for the image; it lifts me, momentarily, even though I am not sure I fully understand it. It lifts me because it is a beautiful thought, because I like the idea of turning myself into a pacifist, instead of a fighter; able to navigate the ebbs and flows, allowing them to play out without drowning me. But I don't want William to think that this condition is a given, a natural, repeating cycle, like the migration. It isn't. I don't want to live with this; I want it to change. I feel the panic rising again at the idea that he might be giving up in the face of this thing, and I fight it down. I focus on my hands again.

I feel ashamed that I can't seize the day. That I haven't been able to steer my way through life by reminding myself of migrating wildebeest. I feel the shame like a boulder in my chest. I think of the naked man on the pavement outside the football stadium in Addis Ababa who carried a boulder on his head. But his was public and visible, and it fitted with his nakedness and his bare feet treading the pavement. The boulder was his penance for his sins. When he sat, he laid down the boulder and rolled out a small square of cloth, and passers-by threw their coins onto it, coins stamped with the Lion of Judah. I never knew what he did, what he could possibly have done, to make him think that he had to suffer that punishment.

William puts his arm around my shoulders and hugs me. I try not to cry, I hold my breath instead. I change the subject; I ask him about his trip down the Omo. Who he is going with and why; for how many days.

Then I pick up the leaflet from the bed next to me. It's the one Dad found on the website of an eating-disorders unit in South London. Last night, after I went to bed, Dad went back into the garden to clear up the odds and ends he had left when he abandoned his work to come and collect me. He stacked the logs in the shed, put away his bicycle, wheeled the wheelbarrow down to the bonfire, then came into the house. He opened his laptop and began searching for help. He is the one who found it, a unit dedicated to helping people like me. None of us knew it existed, knew any such thing existed. He printed off a leaflet from their website and brought it to me.

William and I look at it together.

'Will you contact them?' my brother asks.

'Yes, definitely,' I say.

'I think it's a very good idea,' William says. I turn the leaflet over in my hands.

'Shall I open the curtains?' he asks.

'Yes, please.'

He opens the curtains and light falls onto the bed, onto the matt white of the cupboard and the walls.

When William leaves later that morning I dial the number on the leaflet. I am given an appointment for the following week, with a Professor Lacey, the head of the unit. By mid-morning Anna calls for an update and tells me she can drive me there, to the unit; we can go together.

A week later Anna sits in the coffee-smelling waiting room while Professor Lacey flips peremptorily through a questionnaire I have filled in. That is when he pulls out an envelope and draws the cake with three layers. On the top layer he writes 'B + V', binge and vomit, on the middle layer he writes 'D A A', depression, anxiety and anger, and on the bottom layer he draws messy swirls – the maelstrom, he calls it. I can't take my eyes off the cake, the swirls of the maelstrom, the three layers, on the envelope that sits between us, on the desk with the green trim. I know the Professor is looking at me, impatient, perhaps, to get on, but I am transfixed. He has no idea what a revelation this is. He doesn't know that this is the beginning of the end for me.

It is my first leap forward, this simple diagram. It is my first indication that this is something that can be understood, that has been understood before; it is something that has a logic that can be circumscribed in the roughly sketched black lines of a three-layered cake. A few months later I reproduce the diagram for my family, on my father's flipchart.

Professor Lacey refers me on to a therapist called Penny. I contact her and arrange to meet her at her first available appointment, one week later, at the very end of December.

PART VI:
HOME
2005–2006

Our hut at Lake Langano, Ethiopia.

Twenty-Seven

London. December 2005.
Thirty-one years old

In the waiting room of the unit there is a coffee machine and a fish tank. I press the button and a milky brown liquid spills out into a small paper cup, smelling faintly of UHT milk, which I like. I decide on the sofa along the wall next to the fish tank; there might be neon tetras in there. I can't decide whether to pick up the newspaper or watch the fish. I pick up the paper and lay it down on my lap. There is something about Pakistan on the cover: a photograph of a man in a shalwar khameez in the desert, a strong wind blowing his khameez sideways against his wiry body and a loose end from a cloth turban on his head flying away from him, and next to that a picture of Emmanuelle Béart. Emmanuelle Béart whose small breasts made me feel so unwieldy. I don't want to read the piece about Pakistan or Emmanuelle Béart now, there isn't the time. I need to collect myself, calm myself, before my meeting with Penny.

I peer into the tank to see if there are any neon tetras, the fish we used to buy for our tank at home from the Sarit Centre in Nairobi. On Waiyaki Way there was a dip in the road where we kids in the back of the car would sing the Kenyan national anthem, and it comes back to me, after all these years, as I sit in the waiting room, waiting for Penny.

> 'Oh God of all Creation,
> Bless This Our Land and Nation.'

After the first verse we held our breath – it was the rules – until we'd passed the trees on the other side of the dip, when we were allowed to breathe again and continue:

> 'Justice be our Shield and Defender,
> May We Dwell in Unity,
> Peace and Liberty,
> Plen-ty to be found within our Borders.'

All of us losing time on the last line, stumbling to the last word. We never knew how to sing the last line properly, it had too many words. Even in Swahili the last line sounded rushed. On the way back from the Sarit Centre, holding our neon tetras in plastic bags filled with water, we'd do the same but use our free hand to beat time with our wooden candy-floss sticks, licked clean.

Another girl enters the room, with her parents. The three of them sit on the sofa against the wall adjacent to me. I cannot resist looking at her, at them. Someone else with my problem. I want to stare, but I know I can't. She looks young, she can't be more than eighteen, perhaps twenty, but it's hard to tell. I must

be ten years older than her at least. I wonder how she came to
be here so quickly, so early on in her journey. I wonder what
her disease is, anorexia or bulimia. I ignore the paper, the fish
tank, and hold the paper cup close to my lips, taking small sips
of tea, sneaking glances at her over its rim. I sit still, trying to
hear what they are saying, trying to piece together who they
are, but mostly they aren't talking, they are just sitting, in a still
gap before moving on.

When they do say something it is respectfully hushed. Her
parents are well dressed, I think the father might have a
European accent. German perhaps. He has only said a couple
of words. He looks like a businessman, bringing a halt to the
things going on in his businessman's life elsewhere, in rooms
less still than this one. They do not look self-conscious, so
perhaps they are used to being here. Come to think of it, they
look at ease here. Perhaps she has come here to be an in-patient,
perhaps this isn't her first time. Maybe it's her room I looked
into as I cut around the side of the building. When I arrived I
went to the main building, where my sister had brought me to
meet Professor Lacey, and I was redirected here, to the low, flat
unit for eating disorders. As I crunched across the gravel I'd
looked through a window and seen it was a bedroom. It had a
single bed against the wall, simply made, narrow, a desk, and an
apple on the windowsill. A frugal, pared-down room, a private
room. There was a T-shirt folded neatly on the end of the bed.
I'd looked away quickly, hurried on.

The girl in the waiting room is cool, detached. Her hair is
shiny and washed and long; she wears it in a high ponytail and
dark strands of hair fall over one shoulder. She sits without
fidgeting. She must be an honest person, more honest than I

am, to have told her parents when still so young. She must be unafraid in some way. She must be good at talking, at getting words out, no matter the effect.

The door opens and Penny steps into the room. She says my name. I stand up, push my scarf into my bag, throw my coat over my arm and shake her hand, firmly, look her in the eye, the way we have always been taught. She smiles. Follow me, she says, and I walk behind her down the corridor. She walks without making noise, she is calm and strong. We enter a small plain room and she invites me to sit down in the chair opposite hers. There is a patch of blue carpet between us, a radiator against the wall under a window that looks out onto trees, and a wall beyond the trees. There is a box of tissues on the window ledge, and next to it the dried-out husk of an insect.

The hour passes quickly. We go through the notes she has that Professor Lacey handed on, the grit of things. How often, and for how long. How long it takes, what I typically eat in a binge, how I end the binge. How many years. It takes me a little while to do the maths, working backwards through the years. 94 to 98: Oxford; gap year before that, in 93; which means 91 to 92: boarding school in England. I can't remember if I started immediately so I'll give myself the benefit of the doubt and call it 92. So 2006 minus 1992. Fourteen years.

'It depends how you count it,' I say, to make it sound less bad. Fourteen years sounds theatrical. 'It's had its ups and downs. It started slowly and only got really bad when I went to Oxford.' Penny nods. And then there's a pause. I hope she isn't thinking that I'm a dyed-in-the-wool hopeless case after all these years, that I'm cracked, like my sister's friend Yeshi, who hid with her in the hut when the crazy man attacked them in the asylum. I don't blame her, if she thinks that I'm cracked. And I'm old, compared to the girl in the waiting room. I twist the ring on my middle finger.

Penny and I agree that I will come and see her every week, Monday at 4 p.m., as an outpatient. This will be my time with her, kept for me every week, and I in return have to commit to that time. There is always, she says, the option of coming here as an in-patient. Let's see how we get on, she says.

Then she hands me a small blue notebook, a food diary. On its cover the word 'Confidential' is printed in the top-right corner. She shows me a page, divided into columns for what I eat and when, and a column for comments. She asks me if I'd like to start filling it in, each day. I say yes. I take the notebook eagerly, hold it tightly in my hand. I'll start tonight, I say. I want to show her that I'm keen, I'm going to work hard, I'm going to work so hard.

Penny asks me to bring the notebook with me to each session. She'll keep it to read and give me another, a clean one, each time we meet. Together we can begin to identify patterns. The binge is a marker, she says, which will point to what is going on underneath it. I think of Professor Lacey's cake, the B + V of the top layer.

This has been going on for a very long time, she says.

I nod. Yes, it has, I say.

It's OK, she says. You can cry.

And I feel the last fourteen years expanding out from me, pooling out over the blue carpet, pooling out into the empty space.

I look at Penny and she looks back at me.

On the bus home I sit on the top deck in a window seat, looking

out through the fogged-up window as we approach the low
Hammersmith Bridge. Down on the wintry river pointed boats
and rowers scull smoothly, strongly, appearing and disappearing
through the low mist that hangs down over the river's banks. As
the bus pauses on the bridge I hear the coxes shouting out as the
rowers pull away, pulling with the same rhythm and the same
movement until they disappear from my sight. The bus edges
over the bridge, stopping and starting, stopping and starting.

My hands are buzzing, my chest is buzzing, as if from a low
electrical charge. I feel a space, a physical space, in my head,
opening up between my ears. I feel freed. For in the room I
have just left I have found a place, somewhere I never believed
existed, for my fears and worries and disappointments; a place
where they are understood, where they are recognised, and
where they are known. After all these years I have found somewhere I can lay it all down.

That night I dream I'm on a boat in the middle of a great flat sea.
Dragging behind me is a floating platform of detritus, twisted
bits of old rusting metal, useless containers, rubbish, attached
to my boat by thick ropes. I climb to the back of the boat and
with a knife I start sawing through the ropes. The island of rubbish floats away over the horizon. I turn and there is land ahead
of me, its forests reach down to its shore. I climb off the boat,
and walk.

Twenty-Eight

London. January 2006

With the burnt-off edge of the wooden spoon I scrape the porridge into my bowl, then I cut up a banana on top. Just before the boiling milk spills over the top of the pan I lift it off the uneven coil, glowing orange, spitting and hissing with drops of burnt milk, and pour it into my coffee. I take my breakfast down the corridor and into the living room to the white table under the skylight. It's a weekend, a Saturday morning; the London flat is peaceful.

The blue notebook is in the middle of the table, where I left it last night after I completed my food entries for the day. Notebook number seven. Penny writes the number of the notebook on the front cover before she gives it to me, one each week. So I've been seeing her for seven weeks now, every Monday, without fail.

I open up the notebook as I eat, flatten it down against the table, and fill in the empty columns. In the first column:

9.30 a.m.

Porridge

Banana

Milky coffee

Then, 'Breakfast, in the flat', in the second column.

The last column on the page is for thoughts. 'Comments,' it says, at the top. I lay the pen down and look up, look around me to take a measure of things.

'Saturday morning,' I write. 'I am alone and with a wide-open day ahead of me.'

I take another mouthful of my breakfast and chew slowly, think about where I am, what I am doing, what my thoughts are. I am not working this weekend, I don't know if that is a good thing as it means I have unformed time ahead of me. An open day. The new project I have started with Fran, the Olympics' project, stumbles along, rarely spilling into my free time, into my weekends. So I am free to do whatever I like today. On top of that, I haven't planned much for this weekend, so there is nothing to split it into smaller, more manageable segments of time.

And I am alone. I'd rather not be alone. Perhaps I should have planned to visit my parents this weekend after all, or I should have thought ahead and made plans to see friends. Perhaps I should have booked things in. I pick up a teaspoon and skim the skin of milk from my coffee. It drips a line of brown dots across the table. I lay the spoon down on a saucer.

I turn back to the notebook. 'I would rather not be alone, and I would rather not have a wide-open day,' I write. 'But I am OK. Maybe it's all right just to be OK.'

I pick up my coffee, hold it in both hands, think about what I have written. Perhaps I have put my finger on something; perhaps my expectations of every day are too insistent. I'll talk about it with Penny when I see her on Monday. Perhaps, just for this day, it's OK for it to be neither up nor down, just resting somewhere in the middle, without expectation.

I close the blue notebook, smooth it with the palm of my hand. My familiar blue notebooks. I carry them with me wherever I go, and I fill in the columns every day, at every meal. If I can't fill in the entries for any particular meal, I'll do it at the end of the day, reflecting back on the day and its undulations. It makes me realise how little I stood back, before, and looked calmly, unhurriedly, at the state of things, and at how one thing tipped so easily into another. It makes me see what a powerful thing it is to simply pause, and think, and write. I'll tread carefully today. I want to take it to ten clear days in a row, and I am already at nine.

This morning, I decide, I'll explore the river's embankment, go as far as I can along it, heading east, following the bends and stretches of the Thames. If I'm taken away from the river, I'll loop back again. And later on I'll make sure to set something up for the afternoon, or the evening, with friends; that way the day won't be so open-ended.

At the end of the street I emerge along a path above rows of low, winter-weathered houseboats. I'm walking quickly, head down, trying to reason with the mild anxiety I feel at the day ahead of me, so I hear the helicopter before I see it. It is a news helicopter, hovering high up in the sky between the two bridges. Then I notice small groups of people leaning over the embankment and four builders in fluorescent jackets hanging over the bridge, looking down into the brown, Saturday-flowing river. And then I see it, the shining, unmistakable form of a whale, wallowing in the Thames.

I climb quickly onto the low wall by Battersea Bridge, and settle in to watch the beautiful creature in the water. A rescue operation is already under way. Small boats bob around the whale, boats and flags and yellow jackets industrious against the brown flow, trying to save it. A soft sunlight bounces off its skin. Now I know what will anchor my morning, and anchor me solidly here.

Within an hour small crowds have gathered along the embankments on both sides of the river. Before long, a news crew from Norway appears, next to where I am sitting on the wall, and as the crew sets itself up, the presenter starts practising her piece to camera. I eavesdrop on their conversation. The cameraman is bent over, tying his shoelace with his back to the presenter, but she pays no attention and carries on her lively rehearsal to the unattended camera on its tripod.

I can't take my eyes off the creature below me in the brown waters. How did it end up here, so lost? How did it end up in the heart of this teeming city? Perhaps it was a simple mistake, perhaps in a moment of absent-mindedness it took an unthinking left turn on its way to the North Pole, just a slight deviation from its route along the eastern waters of the British Isles, and found itself all of a sudden in darker and murkier water, channels narrowing around it, the sharp edges of boats reaching out to it, the booming vibrations of a city swamping in from the river's banks.

And then, maybe, out of some misplaced confidence, or

blindness, or fear, it kept on going until it ended up here on my doorstep, rolling, shooting water into the air through its blowhole like the whale in the Jonah story.

The Norwegians' production assistant arrives, smelling of cigarette smoke, carrying a tray of coffees in paper cups with plastic lids. The coffees smell good. He hands them out. He smiles at me and I smile back at him. I straighten up on the wall, tie back my hair. He looks as though he didn't get much sleep last night. I did. I slept well, and I woke with a little skip of joy this morning: another good day yesterday – yesterday was the ninth in a row, that makes today number ten. Number Ten. I take a deep breath, breathe in the aroma of the coffee. Deep in, and out. I drop my shoulders, arch my back, stretch, look around me at the clear sky.

The sky over the South London houses is a clear, wintry blue. Blue sky. Penny said it was OK to mourn the old days, all that time, all that wasted blue sky. It came back to me, spectral-like, when in Penny's room I finally allowed it its existence. I did mourn. It came seeping up like the water table through sodden soil, unstoppable. I'd wake in the night, feverish, with a pure pre-conscious sorrow seeping upwards and upwards, not knowing whose pain it was, it could have been anyone's. The days were long and difficult; underneath everything I felt exhausted and sick, with a heaviness I couldn't shake. The idea of the blue sky haunted me, now that I had let it out into the clear air.

But even while I mourned, there were clumps of wellness, stretching and shrinking like jellyfish, three days here, five days there, once a full seven days clear. And now these, these nine, full, unbroken days of clear eating, of note-taking, of calm and determined focus.

The pockets of wellness began immediately after my first meeting with Penny. I walked out of the low unit after our first meeting a different person, with a charge flowing from the ends of my fingers. I've slowed. I am powerful. I am careful, methodical in my note-taking in the blue diaries she gives me, and that focus, that forced awareness, has seeped out into my behaviour.

By observing and writing I force myself to pause, to think, to take the measure of the impulse when it comes to me, to notice the thoughts I have through the day, and it has been an extraordinary awakening. I have fallen asleep knowing I have, for that day, won, and woken each morning exhilarated, touching my stomach, running the tip of my tongue along the insides of my cheeks, knowing that I did it again: I won again. But there have also been days of a strained, grey vigilance, a thick-headed, anxious wading through the day, and I fall into bed exhausted and emptied out, but safe. And then there are still the bad days, when I feel I can't fight it, I can't win.

The whale rolls, shoots water into the air and the group of builders on the bridge let out a cheer. The rescuers on boats are going to try to tow her out to deeper water in the Thames Estuary east of us, flowing out into the deep waters of the North Sea, pull her back to where she came from and hope she finds her way from there.

I can't see her eyes from here, tiny whale eyes on their sea of whale skin, swivelling like a chameleon's between the Boy with a Dolphin at the Albert Bridge and the cast-iron arches of Battersea Bridge down here where I am. She is so beautiful, all soft curves and shining skin and slowness, and still blowing water in hopeful streams into the air.

I touch the inside of my cheeks with my tongue, feeling the soft underbelly of my mouth. I know it would be easy to let go today, to abandon the vigilance, let myself be pulled in, back under. I imagine straightening up, flexing, on the low embankment wall; and then a perfect Kenyan top board, swallow-dive into the water, a graceful arc, touch my toes, straighten out and barely a splash as I enter next to the whale's gleaming flanks.

So tempting to let go. The warmth of it, the familiarity, the safe downness, a soft cover settling over all the sharp edges, over whatever I want to ward off. But I won't do it, not today. Perhaps some other day, taken unawares.

I rub my hands together, dig in my bag for my gloves. I'd like a cup of tea to warm my fingers, and something to eat, something to keep me going before lunch. Breakfast was a few hours ago now. I could be back at the flat in minutes and bring a couple of biscuits back on a plate. I'd enjoy a cup of tea and a thoughtful biscuit here on the wall, with the whale. I will sit here for a long time, and watch her. I will eat both biscuits slowly, consciously, to stop the swallow dive. I will write in the blue notebook, commit the biscuits to paper, write down my thoughts in the Comments column, pin it down.

I'll get to the heart of anything that way. Sometimes it is the simplest thing.

It always comes from somewhere, Penny said, and to my utter amazement I have discovered that it is true. I can trace it back, on the bad days, in the blue diaries, in simple analysis with Penny, to some trigger *outside of myself* to which I am reacting. It isn't me; it is just the interface between me and the outside. I am not cracked, like Yeshi, like the crazy man with the stick. It does always come from somewhere, from whatever it might be:

from feeling undermined or sidelined, from the fear of some strange and overblown loneliness that I have built up in my head, from a frustrating hour, an unsatisfying conversation, from wanting to wipe away the day or ward off disappointment, in myself, in other people, from not wanting to face up to any of the stuff I don't want to. All ordinary stuff, it turns out.

And because that *somewhere* exists, outside of myself, it is also within my power to alter it. It is within my power to alter my own response to it, if nothing else. Nine unbroken days have taught me that I can be a powerful foe against this bully.

Now, the impulse itself is my warning sign that something is amiss. I seek it out now, pin it down, when it comes to me. It doesn't always work, it often doesn't, but I'm getting better and better at it. When it doesn't work, I look at it with Penny, at the day, at the thoughts and feelings that preceded the binge, and with her help we look at the pieces of the bigger picture. We try to fit them together in a more objective light.

Yes, I'll go back to the flat now, and bring the tea and the biscuits back with me. I'll come back to the same spot with the Norwegians. I'll open the notebook on my knee and write down '2 Marie Biscuits', and I'll think. That way I'll be safe: in the pause, in the thoughtful gap, I know I will be saved.

Twenty-Nine

At my parents' home in Sussex.
April 2006

Penny advised patience. It isn't easy to let go completely, she said, of something that has served a purpose, however destructive, for so many years. It was hard to be patient. Though in the first months after meeting her the number of episodes dropped away dramatically, they didn't disappear altogether. Each time it happened again, I felt crushed. I felt I was starting again from the beginning.

Penny told me that some eating-disordered patients think they are going to miss the thrill of the binge. For me it wasn't the thrill of the binge itself, it was the thrill of what the binge represented. It was the thrill of my secret get-out-of-jail-free card, the relief that accompanied the nihilistic freedom of granting myself permission to abandon ship, to relinquish any responsibility, to myself or to others or to the world. The binge was my opportunity to spectacularly let go, to disappear, to duck out of an ordinary reality.

I began to fear the long weeks and months of vigilance. Would I always have to think so carefully, be so aware, be ready at all times to defend myself against the impulse when it came? Would that impulse ever go away? Yes, it would go away, Penny said.

She encouraged me to think of it like a wave, a physical wave. I should ride it out, let it turn to nothing. An impulse comes, but it also goes if you wait long enough. But that didn't work for me, it was too painful. Trying to stay on the wave as the impulse came to me was agonising. What did work for me was the thoughtfulness, the rare detachment, that lay behind picking up my pen and writing in the blue notebook – sometimes that simple act was enough to smash it to nothing. But that didn't always work either.

I felt flattened, disheartened by a smattering of bad days I'd had the previous month. I needed a break from London, from work and routine, after a couple of difficult and disappointing weeks. Work continued as normal. Fran and I stumbled along on the Olympics' project, which felt often as if it was going nowhere, and I began working with another director, Ben, filming a lifer who had recently come out of prison in Manchester. It was after a series of days in Manchester that I decided to go back to my parents' home. I knew Anna would be there too, for the weekend.

It was during that weekend, early on the Saturday morning as I made my bed, absently, in the peace of the countryside morning, stringing together in my head the words of a Spanish song about María la Portuguesa down by the river, when Dad slipped out of the house and cycled through the promising spring air, past the empty speed camera on the outskirts of the village, which had flashed him regularly when they first came back from Africa before he understood what it was. He cycled past the pub, past the post office, to the village stationer's to buy a flipchart.

He'd have consulted Mum about the flipchart first. Mum, the arbiter of family sensitivities, hoped that the flipchart, on balance, was a good idea. They would like some answers, Dad had said, on a walk we'd taken along a field of new maize. They'd like some explanation, some insight, since by then I had been seeing Penny for three months, and three months seemed long enough to settle on some answers. They would like to understand it better, Dad said, so they could help more effectively.

We'd marched down the lane, *left, right, left, right,* over the stile and along the hilltop in our wellington boots after the morning rain, wide sky above us, the cluster of beech trees of Chanctonbury Ring to the south and east of us, and, emboldened by the wind and the sky, I'd said yes, I thought I could do that. Yes, I could try to provide some answers.

But faced with the flipchart in the kitchen I could think of nothing more to offer than the cake with three layers that Professor Lacey, the consultant at the unit, had drawn for me when I first met him. I knew there was more, much more, that I could tell them, and I hoped that one day I would be able to explain more clearly. But I hadn't got it straight in my own head, not yet, not enough to be able to put it in plain words.

That night, my father printed out the notes from the family summit and slipped them under my door in a plastic sleeve. I sat on the edge of my bed and read through them in the light cast by the bedside lamp. The notes ran to four pages. After the

Environmental Factors Before and Now were detailed, he summarised with a recap of our family commitment to Be Positive to DEFOE, and the words 'Caroline has made it clear that she is the only one who can make herself better.' Two spaces, then: 'We must all be patient.'

The next morning I wake to the sound of wood pigeons in the garden, and their sound is light and promising. I think back to the day before. Thanks to my father, we have taken the next step, the step I should have allowed to happen years ago after I first told my family about my illness in Uganda. It wasn't as bad as I thought it would be, the family discussion. We managed to touch on things that might have been difficult, and it didn't all fall apart. The things that nod to an idea we don't usually subscribe to – that there is room for self-pity, room for a circumspect look at our choices, even in the midst of all that we have and all that we have always had, even in the midst of the far greater suffering of others.

I want to be outside. I pull on my trainers and call the dog. We run out into the countryside together, up the hill to the old, empty church that every year looks more a part of the field in which it sits. We run across the fields. We don't get lost this time. We run and run, and charge down a pock-marked, uneven field to an old oak that Anna and I like to cycle to. I sit under it, my back against its trunk, the damp earth soaking into my shorts and the grass prickling my legs, and out here, under the tree, under a sweep of oak branches and sky, the euphoria of the ten-day stretch of wellness comes back to me, and the two-week stretch of wellness, and I feel the strength and the clarity of those days coming back to me again. And I know that this is how it will be for some time. There will be ups and downs; it will take time.

You have to be patient, Penny said. The key to recovery is in understanding, understanding what is going on, and then gradually building a different, more objective, picture of your-self, because in the course of the illness you lose sight of who you are.

Here, under the tree, and in the euphoria of the run and the fresh air, I feel the clarity of perspective clearing a space around me, seeping down to me through the gullies of the trunk, and I see that my recent bad days are nothing more than that, nothing more than blips in longer and longer periods of wellness. Because in spite of how it has felt recently, I know that I am getting better, and I know that today I can bring it back within my control. I have the blue notebooks to slow it down, to reduce it, to pin it down, and I have the fundamental understanding that I can change this, with Penny's help. Everything has already changed; everything has shifted.

The dog licks me, flattening the hairs of my forearm, and I scratch his head. He flops his head onto my lap, so my thighs settle further into the damp soil and grass. After some time I shift him off me and stand and stretch against the tree, and we run up out of the field and back down the lane, past the dip, past the bridge over the stream, past the gate that opens to a meadow of long grass and wild flowers, past the barn and the horses, to the wooden gate of the driveway. Dad is there, back at work, scraping away at the soft, rotted wood of the planks of the log shed, his gardening sweater and his hair sprinkled with bits of stick and leaf.

'Tea, Dad?' I call to him.

'Yes, please,' he says. 'I'll be in in a minute.'

I go into the kitchen and put the kettle on. In the middle of the table sits the cake from the bread bin, spilling a trail of yellow crumbs off its plate across the faded pine. It's the cake they didn't want to bring out yesterday, just in case, but now I look at it in the coherent light of mid-morning after a run, and it is nothing – nothing more than a cake. I'll have some when the tea is ready.

I look at the flipchart, it is still in the kitchen. It's open at 'Factors from Childhood'. There is Lin, second bullet point down, my childhood friend from Pakistan. She lives in America now. She lives with her girlfriend and teaches at the University of Missouri. We haven't really spoken for years. But she called, out of the blue, perhaps a year ago, and told me that she was driving her car one day, from Missouri to Virginia where she was visiting her parents, and she suddenly, in a moment, realised that she had finally said goodbye, to me, and to that old life. She realised, she said, that she had finally 'got over it'. I imagine her in an open-topped car, her face broader now, her black hair tied back, her hands steady on the wheel, her movements certain and assured, as something floats up, out of her chest, up into the swirling air above the car, above the fields and the endless road, spiralling up, up, up into the sky and away.

Anna comes into the kitchen and we hug, leaning heavily against each other, and resting our heads on one another's shoulders, as we often do when we greet each other. I make Anna a cup of tea, and one for Dad, then we both sit, side by side at the end of the table, looking at the flipchart, laughing about Pakistan, about how embarrassed we were to have British accents at our new American international high school in Islamabad. In the restaurant of the hotel we were living in while my parents looked for a house to rent, we'd tiptoe in the mornings past the American family helping themselves liberally to the buffet breakfast, parathas and papaya and scrambled eggs. We'd have eaten our breakfast in the hotel room before we came downstairs, tea and a dry pound cake Mum bought in the market, a more economical kind of breakfast. Outside on the road we'd wait with our schoolbags in our high-top trainers – Anna's black, mine yellow – for the real, yellow American school bus that collected us for school.

'Do you think they imported those buses from America?' Anna asks me.

'No, surely not,' I say.

'Well, they imported their orange juice,' she says. 'Remember the American commissary?' We laugh. We'd have loved to have been allowed into the American commissary, a wonderland of imported and packaged foods in a corner of the American compound with its swimming pool and movie screen, in the north of the city.

Dad comes in then and joins us so we are all three balancing on the end of the table, looking at the flipchart, drinking tea, talking about Pakistan, about the war over the border in Afghanistan and the rugs we bought at the Friday market woven with images of Kalashnikovs and tanks, next to the Saddam Hussein-faced watches, and the cages of live chicks dipped in bright dyes. And then we are just sitting, companionably, looking at the flipchart.

'Weren't we lucky?' Dad says.

'Yes,' I say. 'I wouldn't change it for anything.'

'Shame your mother isn't here,' Dad says. 'She's missing out.'

Mum will be on her way back from church by now. If she were here, she'd be sitting between us, right in the middle, arms linked. She hates to miss out on an opportunity for story-telling.

Dad stands up to go back to the garden, but before he leaves he indicates the flipchart with a sweep of his arm. 'I hope it was some help, all this,' he says.

'Yes, it was. Thanks, Dad,' I say. He squeezes my arm.

'It was a good illustration of the cake,' he says. 'I thought that was very interesting, the different layers feeding into each other. The idea of a maelstrom of life underneath it all. Quite poetic, really.'

'It was,' agrees Anna. 'I wonder if Professor Lacey knows about Be Positive to DEFOE,' she laughs. 'Maybe you should tell him about it if you see him again.'

Dad cuts each of us a slice of cake with a blunt table knife, spreading more crumbs across the table. He doesn't bother with sharp knives or plates – why waste time when he could be outside, working in the garden, on a day like this.

Thirty

London. June 2006

'Yes, I think you should,' says Hugh. 'Why not?'

'That's what I think,' I say. I have the phone wedged between my ear and my shoulder as I navigate around the Internet dating site on my desktop computer at work. 'And it might be fun too. I'm not going to spend long writing up the bit about myself, I just want to put it out there and see what happens. I don't want to get neurotic about it, or spend lots of time doing it.'

I straighten up and pull myself towards my desk on my chair with wheels. The cleaner is here, the Mexican one today, with her bucket and mop, and she's running a cursory damp cloth over the desks and telephones. I pull in so she can get to the desk behind me.

'*Hola*,' I mouth at her, and she smiles at me.

'Have you got a good picture?' Hugh asks.

I look at the picture I've pulled up on my computer screen, the one I have chosen for my profile page. I'm in a striped bikini, on a beach, last summer. Alex sent it to me recently with a one-line message saying he'd always liked the picture and thought I might like to have it. I haven't seen him since we split up a year ago but I get the occasional, succinct message.

You can only see the top of me in the picture, and I'm smiling. I look happy, healthy, rounded.

'I think so. It'll do. Only thing is I'm in a bikini. You can't see much, but I'm not sure . . .'

'Do it,' Hugh says. 'Bikini is a good idea.'

I laugh.

'I'd better get on with it. I want to send it and get home before it starts to bucket down. I'm on my bike.'

As I hang up the phone the first fat drops of June rain splash against the windows, against the windscreens of the cars lining up on the Westway heading out of the city in the uncertain summer light. I glance down at them, briefly wondering where they are headed, to country tracks and gardens and wildlife, the smell of grass and earth. Then I look back to the profile and finish writing it as quickly as I can.

'*Buenas noches,*' the cleaner calls as she carries her bucket and mop past me and through the swing doors to another part of the floor. As she walks, the banks of lights on the ceiling flicker back to life. Most of the floor is unlit as we are the last ones here.

I wave my hand over my head to relight the bank of lights above me, and quickly read through what I've written. It seems close enough to one of any number of likenesses of myself – to the way I perceive them, anyway. And to what I look for in a partner. I have never thought about it in this way. I like thinking about what I want. Men have always liked me, I have always had boyfriends, but they have just happened to me, on the whole, in an unthinking kind of way.

This way, I am thinking about what *I* would like, I am asserting myself, thinking it through, sculpting something out of nothing, and I like that. It feels a stronger, more decided way of doing things. I read it through one more time. I'd like someone who would be happy to bring me a cup of tea while I'm reading. That would be a good start. Someone who would happily lay a place at the table for a goat, if a goat came round for tea. What I mean by the goat is that I'd like the other person to be open-minded, to be instinctively, approvingly generous towards the world – but I think it may be a bit obscure. Never mind, it's fine, it's not too serious, nor boastful. I submit the profile to the website, and shut down.

I pack up my bits and pieces into my bag and lock the most recent tapes from our Olympics' filming into the rushes cupboard. I address a large manila envelope to Chris, our lifer in Manchester, and place it in the mail tray. I'm sending him back the notes he lent us, the notes on his case from the Crown Prosecution Service, because Ben and I won't be going back to Manchester. Our editor pulled the lifer film. He said he didn't believe anything was really going to happen after prison, anything with a strong enough narrative for our audience, not within our timeframe; and though Ben and I both argued against it, he was probably right. Ben has moved on to another project outside the BBC. He seemed relieved to go, and Chris and his Mum in Manchester didn't seem to mind too much either.

I walk quickly to the lifts as the ceiling lights flicker on around me. In the lift I stand close to the mirror and stare at my reflection, at my green eyes, at my mouth, at my hair. My face looks different to me lately. It seems stronger, and more defined, brighter than I remember it. I lost sight of it for a few weeks, but the buzzing feeling has come back to me: the low, energetic, electric hum that I felt so vividly after my first meeting with Penny. It came back to me the day after the flipchart, and it hasn't gone, and I don't need to look at my eyes, at the still, determined mouth in the lift's mirror, to know that it is there.

Harish is at the other turnstiles, the ones for people entering the building, and I call out to him.

'Night, Jonesy,' he calls back. 'I hope you have your raincoat today.' He tugs at his belt, shifts his position. He didn't get the marketing job he applied for, but he'll keep applying. I know he'll manage it. He says he's going to leave this job anyway; he's had enough of standing at the turnstiles all day.

'Want me to wait for you?' I ask him. 'I'll walk with you to the tube.'

'Nah. You're too fast for me,' he says.

I cycle quickly down Wood Lane and cut across Shepherd's Bush Green on the cycle lane, past the tramps drinking cider on the bench, their faces leathery and brown from the first weeks of summer. Harish is right, I'm fast tonight. As I reach the residential streets of Olympia the heavens open, but I don't stop to zip up my raincoat; instead I stand up on the pedals and cycle as fast as I can into the rain. By the time I emerge onto the Hammersmith Road I'm already drenched.

Red double-deckers are backed up all the way to the top of the North End Road, the street a sea of brake lights and smeared windows, the smell of exhaust fumes and pavement. I stop abruptly behind a bus, with one foot in a puddle, and feel the water soaking up through a split corner of my Green Flash. The fronts of my jeans, tight on my thighs, are soaked through. I inch to the side of the bus, peer around it, judging whether I can risk passing it through the middle of the traffic. Once I'm past this blockage I'll head east and cut through Brompton Cemetery; I'll fly through the cemetery.

I know I am not going to lose it tonight. I even know what I am going to eat. I have the food in the bag on my back. I shift the rucksack into the middle of my back and lean further around the side of the bus. I don't need to wait behind these elephantine machines, grunting in the rain. I pull out into the middle of the road to get past the bus, then swing in front of it and mount the pavement, cutting back into the road ahead of the traffic just as the lights turn green. There is a roar as a mass of buses and cars surge forward behind me.

That's when I see the man from the curry house, through a chaos of raindrops and car lights, bending over the glass cabinet, a ghost in white – hot curry, hot, steaming curry – but I'm past so quickly he doesn't even look up. 'NO!' I shout into the rain. 'NO!' This is war, a joyful battle I am going to win. 'NO!' I shout again, laughing at the rain, at the mired traffic, so fast, so fast nobody can catch me.

Brompton Cemetery is empty in the rain and the evening's half-light. I'm fast, I'm back on my chopper, cycling to the giraffe pond with my jar for collecting tadpoles, hoping today I'll see the Cape buffalo that stood in my brother's path here yesterday. I'm in control of my destiny. A man and a dog are in the cemetery but I'm past them so fast they barely see me. I'm a shadow, a spirit flying between the headstones, tilting left, tilting right, the mud from a brown puddle splashes up to reach me. I know where the cemetery leads. I know this patch: this is my patch. This is my patch as much as it is the man's and the dog's, my road as much as it is the bus driver's, who raised his fist as I cut in front of him. I'm past the domed chapel, past the headstones reaching to me futilely through the rain, and out through the southern gates.

I dismount outside the flat, carry my bike down the stone steps and lock it to the Victorian railings.

Home. I hang up my raincoat in the hallway and glance into my room on my way down the corridor towards the living room. My bed is made, the plump blue-covered duvet spread evenly across the bed, the curtains wide open. In the kitchen I unzip my rucksack and place the chicken pieces and the bag of salad leaves on the counter. On the draining board sit my bowl and saucepan and spoon from breakfast, the wooden spoon with the burnt edge. I catch sight of the blackbird who spends time in the patio garden, one of my uncle's companions when he is here. I've forgotten the blackbird's name. My uncle will be back in a few weeks and I will move out. I'll send him a message to let him know the blackbird is still here and doing well.

The dimpled skin on the chicken curls up in the hot oil, shrivelling away from the fat thighs. I run to my room, peel off my muddy jeans, pull a sweater over my head and tie my wet, tangled hair in a knot on the top of my head. I wipe at the mascara under my eyes with my fingertips, then I run back to the kitchen in time to see holes appear between the simmering rice grains; it is ready. I take the pine nuts out of the oven, already burnt around their edges, and scatter them over the salad, pour olive oil and vinegar over it, salt, add a few more cubes of feta. On the side of the plate a big dollop of crushed chillies in oil, the red oil seeping outwards. I carry my plate and the pot of chillies to the table. I cut open the thigh, it falls open, succulent, spilling its juice into the red oil. I open the blue diary to today, and write.

'Chicken, salad, rice etc.,' I write. In the middle column: 'Normal meal.' In the right-hand column: 'I have had a calm, focused day. Two more days and I will have gone three weeks without a binge.'

I leave the diary open next to me. This is what I do now; it is an automatic association: when I eat, I think. I clear my head, assess where I am. After five months of this it is now an ingrained habit. It keeps me lucid, it keeps me thinking; it stops the music changing without me noticing.

I slice off an end of chicken with a gnarled bit of skin, push on some rice, dip it in the chillies, crush a cube of feta onto the end of the fork, and eat. My mind wanders. I see myself as if from the outside, as if I am in a film and there I am, eating, calmly, slowly; there I am – pull outwards – in a basement flat on a South London road; pull outwards again – the Thames River, the World's End Estate, the Lots Road Power Station: two beautiful, towering chimneys, beautiful and without purpose, like Battersea Power Station. Then I come back to myself. The power station vanishes. Is it Henry? Is that what my uncle calls the blackbird?

I'll be moving soon. That's easy enough. Most of my possessions should fit into the back of my car with the seats down. I'll take some summer leave, go back to my parents' home, travel with them to Spain for a couple of weeks, then find another room to rent in London. I won't live alone next time. I'll find somewhere near the BBC, near enough to walk. Shepherd's Bush perhaps. There's a market there full of Pakistanis, Arabs, Africans, even a solitary Palestinian with a falafel van. I'm tired of living alone. I'd like to live with friends next time. And I'd like to meet someone.

I cut off more chicken, wonder briefly if I should have fried the other piece. I'll fry it if I'm still hungry. My thoughts flit to the conversations I have with Penny, as they often do. I have been seeing her for five months now, every Monday, meeting in the calm of her room to talk and assess and reflect. Through her, and in the longer and longer periods of time without bingeing, I have been able to learn simple things about myself and about my environment, about what I can and can't control. The last time Penny and I met we talked about a particularly assertive friend who had visited me in London. The friend had talked at me for hours, and then left, and as soon as she had left I had binged. It became clear to me very quickly, in just a few minutes of detached thoughtfulness with Penny, that this friend had me down as someone she could use in this way, as someone she could talk at for hours, on whom she could pour out her stress and her anxieties. She had me down as someone who always listened and didn't have the need to respond.

That was my responsibility, Penny pointed out. I had probably always performed that role for her, so why would she think any different? That would only change if I changed my own behaviour.

'The only person whose behaviour you can control is your own,' Penny said, and I have been mulling it over for days, this simple, powerful truth. All I can control is my own response, my own reaction to the world around me, to the people around me. I can set down my own boundary if I choose, spin it out of the space around me, demonstrate it in my own behaviour, and the rest will follow.

I'd told Penny I could imagine what my mother would say to the story of the girl who visited: 'Put yourself in her shoes,' my mother would say. 'She needs your help; she doesn't seem very happy, she needs someone like you to talk to.' And my mother is right too. But I can't be as selfless as my mother, I know that now. I need to assert myself, to look after myself first, to build myself up. I need to be able to step out of other people's shoes, and step into my own, so that I am solid, and real.

I sit back in my chair, thinking. It is only my own behaviour that I can hope to change, and from that, everything else will alter, rippling outwards.

I push my plate aside and sit still for a while, looking around the room, the dry room with the summer rain drawing to an end outside. I feel it coming; I feel the unfamiliar sensation growing inside me before I recognise what it is. Everything is in the same place. Here I am: I am alone. The room is warm, watched over by the painting of my Irish great-grandmother. She looks like a peaceful woman, a handsome woman. My mother says I look like her. Wedged into the frame next to her is a picture of my uncle's one-eyed cat, Eric. Rain splashes onto the skylight above my head, but I am dry. Nothing, externally, has changed.

And then it comes to me: the absence of fear, the absence of tyranny, in this moment. This is peace, I realise. This is what peace feels like.

Thirty-One

At my parents' home in Sussex.
July 2006

'Good walk?' Mum calls out from the study, and I go to find them.

Dad is at his desk, holding one of my books up against the light streaming in from the window; I asked him this morning if he could fix its fraying spine. My mother is standing behind him, watching photographs appear then fade from the large flat screen of the computer.

'It was beautiful,' I say.

'Were there any Welsh Blacks in the field next to the church today?' Dad asks.

'No, no cows. Just a couple of interested sheep.'

The two sheep had stood at the edge of the field and stared at us, the dog and me, with a simple curiosity. We'd stayed for a while, by the farmer's wooden gate, on the crest of the hill with them, the buzz of insects in the grass, the wind in the tall trees, watching one another, enjoying the simple exchange in the field next to the ancient church.

I stand next to Mum, our arms linked, and watch the pictures on the screen with her. The pictures are set to a permanent slide show when the computer is dormant, so scenes from our lives appear randomly and fade away again, disregarding any linear passing of time. Often the computer picks up only on some peripheral detail of the photograph, imbuing it with a surprising significance. We are looking at an old stretched shoe on a dust-covered foot on a mountain path. I recognise the foot – it's the foot of a boy who sold us honey near Gondar, a town in the north of Ethiopia. He'd offered us the honeycomb, still warm from the tree, dripping honey, speckled with dead bees. He'd sat on a rock, watching, in no hurry to go anywhere, and I'd wondered how long he had been a honey collector, and whether that was what he would always be, and I wonder whether, even now, he is in the mountains near Gondar, wearing the same shoes, stretched longer and wider over time, climbing trees, collecting honey, continuing his solitary and mostly silent life. Then the shoe fades to a hand by the side of a man outside an old English church. This is closer to home, the church looks like the one in a village across the fields from here.

Dad turns the book over in his hands, his head tilted back so he can see through the bottom of his half-glasses. Beyond his head a picture of his own father appears. I look at my father in profile. The strong nose and jaw, the thick brown hair he inherited from his Welsh father. His father is kneeling, in the picture, knees in the grass, thick thighs below football shorts, the picture of strength and health. He was a professional footballer for Wells City, played rugby and cricket and tennis, a sportsman like my own father. He loved to sing. But he died of cancer when he was forty-eight and my own father was only twenty-one. Dad, at twenty-one, was away fighting with the British Army in a jungle in Borneo. One of his units consisted of a patrol of Gurkhas, and his role at night – in fact, probably his most important role, he'd told us – was to sleep close to Captain Damarbahader, the lead Gurkha, by the embers of the fire, close enough so that he could quickly reach out to shake him awake when he shouted out in his nightmares. The other Gurkhas were too respectful to do such a thing themselves even though his cries put all their lives in danger from the enemy fighting them in the jungle. Captain Damarbahader was awarded two Military Crosses for his bravery.

The other thing we know about that war is that Dad kept a pet armadillo in the jungle, as well as a snake and a chicken. The snake liked to keep its body warm curled up in the back of my father's shirt, but also liked to be able to see what was going on, so in the picture I have seen of the four of them, all you can see of the snake is its little pointed head on top of Dad's shoulder. When Dad looked left, the snake looked left, Dad told us; when he looked right, the snake looked right.

The image on the screen is replaced by one of my sister, brother and me on a red murram track. My sister and I are wearing only underpants, speckled blue, and beside the red road is a white rhino with his back to us, head down in the grass. My sister is posing with her hand on her hip. We have the bodies of little gymnasts.

'That must be Meru, in Kenya,' Mum says.

'Why are Anna and I only wearing pants?' I ask.

'I don't know,' Mum says. 'You must have been swimming.'

Dad is stretching out a length of green gaffer tape as Abeji appears on the screen. First we see his worn boots, the same garden boots he wore every day for four years. Then the picture scans over his old blue overalls, over a strong, spare body, to his face under a flat cap. He was our elderly handyman and gardener in Ethiopia. He had a hole in his forehead from childhood, where another child threw a stone at him. My father might have been Abeji in another life, or the other way around. I sometimes thought that Abeji and Dad must be the same person. Abeji was invincible, in spite of his age. He was always fixing things with bits of twine and wood, fixing the bicycles, cutting back the trees, at his own resolute but gentle pace, and at lunchtime he told stories, sitting on a stool in the backyard near the kitchen, eating his *shero wot*, while Tsige and Alganesh listened. Abeji was deeply religious, as was Tsige. They told stories of snakes coming from the mouths of children when they were dipped in the river, freeing them from the Devil. They had seen it with their own eyes.

Dad smoothes down the tape on the spine of the book with the ends of his fingers, eases out the wrinkles so the tape is stretched tight against the cover, then holds it up to appraise it again in the light from the window facing out over the soft afternoon-garden, out there where the Nepali tree with the elephant legs stands. It's *Slouching Towards Bethlehem*, the book Christine lent me nearly a year ago, before we began filming the Alzheimer's documentary with her and her daughter. I need to return it to Christine when I next see her. She is in a home now, and in a contented phase of her Alzheimer's. I've seen her once since she moved to the home, and she no longer knew who I was, but she chatted amiably nonetheless. I told her, over tea and biscuits in the communal garden, that the film had been nominated for a prestigious television award, but that meant nothing to her. She couldn't remember we had ever made a film about her, or why we would.

'Good as new,' Dad says. He lays the book on the desk and turns to me.

'How's Penny's therapy going?' he asks.

'It's going well, thanks, Dad. Really well.' I look at him levelly. I am straight, I am honest. More seas of days when I have felt in control. The red circles have not disappeared from my calendar, but month by month there are fewer and fewer.

'Good news,' Dad says. He lays his hand on the book, fixed, held together, the green tape neat along its spine.

'Has she provided any answers yet?'

'Not really,' I say. 'No magic answer. It's funny. Penny says people always ask for a magic answer. Everyone wants one, I want one, but there never is one. It's more . . .' I hesitate, unsure how to describe it. Sometimes it seems so simple, a series of simple corrections to the picture, adjustments to the colour, the grade, a change of focus here and there. And other times not, other times it feels like a momentous battle against my self.

'It's more,' I say, 'shades of grey. Some big and some smaller realisations, and gradual changes to behaviour, and it all builds. The biggest thing for me was seeing that it does come from somewhere, after all. It has a logic, which changes everything, and which I never understood. It can be pinned down, which means I can work on it and I can change it.'

Out in the garden a woodpecker hammers, and we all pause to listen to it. It fades away.

'But it isn't that simple to explain. There isn't one answer.

Sorry, Dad, it's not that easy to give answers. Not yet.' Dad nods. He understands.

On the wall of the study near his head his old flying goggles are hanging from a nail, unused for many years now. There's a silvery thread of cobweb dangling down from them. I want to reach out and wipe it off.

'I told her about DEFOE,' I say.

Dad laughs.

'I hope you remembered the Be Positive part of it. The most important part of all.'

'I did,' I say. 'Be Positive to DEFOE.'

Again the woodpecker from the garden, working, working at the tree.

'Being positive,' Dad says. 'The only person I know who is consistently positive is your mother.'

Mum laughs. She is beaming.

'And what did Penny think of DEFOE?' Mum asks.

'She said it's important,' I say. 'All that stuff is very important. Diet, exercise and so on. But she said it is peripheral.'

Peripheral. That was the very word she used. And it seemed just right, just the right word. Spinning around on the periphery of some other core. The wildebeest, the DEFOEs, have circled around the periphery, dipping and gliding over the maelstrom, scattering water over bush fires, but it turns out they weren't enough, not for this.

'And I think she's right,' I say, although it feels disloyal. 'I think it's probably the first time I've allowed myself to accept that at the heart of this is something beyond what I can simply control with . . .' – I search for the word – 'with self-discipline, or with being positive. It's more about understanding it, where

it comes from, why it's happening, the layers on Professor
Lacey's cake, the one feeding into the next, I suppose. And
then working to change it.'

There's something else but I can't put my finger on it. Some
other shift happening on the blue carpet, rippling out, beyond
the gate, over the wall, across the river, spreading outward and
ever outward. And then, in the still, calm air of the study Dad
shakes his head.

'I'm afraid you take after me,' he says. 'I have always had to
work to be positive.' I see his strong hand over the back of his
chair. 'I believe that the default human condition is to have a
resting place that is slightly low. I know that I do.'

Dad nods again, lost in his thoughts.

'In fact,' he continues, 'there are times when I feel stuck in
something like a grey fog, and I find it very hard to get out of it.
I know it should be within my power to get out of it, but
somehow I don't or can't.'

I know what he means, of course I do. And I see in his eyes
what it takes to admit to something like this, to owning up to
something that is beyond even his control. Then he turns back
to the desk, picks up the book and hands it to me, smiling.

'But I also know that the reward for making the effort to be
positive comes back in multiples.'

He nods towards the book. 'Good as new. And thank
God you found Penny. She really is excellent. Keep going,
Daughter.'

I take the book back to my bedroom. Dad returns to the
garden, Mother stays a moment longer, caught by the pictures
on the screen. As I leave the room I see my brother, a round,
blond baby, in a bucket with his baby friend Chinelu, the

daughter of our night watchman. Mum is shaking her head. 'Poor baby,' she says.

The photograph was taken in the garden of my parents' home in Enugu, the capital of Biafra. When they arrived in Enugu after Nigeria's civil war, the city, deserted during the war, had already reverted to bush. Mum was the first white woman to return. That is where she fell in love with Africa, she says. My parents were very happy there. But the baby, Chinelu, died from convulsions a few months after they left.

I hold the book in my hand, sit on the end of my bed, look at the matt white of the cupboard. Compassion. That is the word I was looking for in the study; that is the shift. Compassion, not just for Chinelu in the bucket, or the boy with the dusty legs selling a honeycomb full of curled bees. Compassion for myself. The more I did it, the more proof I had that I was a loathsome person. So the next time it came along I fell back, subconsciously, into that recognition of myself as broken, as to blame. But now, somehow, in Penny's room, on the blue carpet, the behaviour and the self have riven apart.

Beyond the old wooden frames of my bedroom window I see my father crossing the garden with the wheelbarrow. I go to the window. His garden companion, the robin who appears beside him while he works, flutters down to the grass and hops about hopefully, waiting for worms. From somewhere comes the low hum of a single-engined plane and I see him glance up into the blue sky, to cumulonimbus cloud and sun glinting off white wings, and I hear the long-ago hum building to a roar as his Cessna crests the eucalyptus trees of our Kenya garden. As the plane roared overhead, Dad would tilt its left wing down and there he was, wearing his pilots' headphones, smiling at us, at the dogs barking up at him.

'Again! Again!' we'd shout at the sky. 'Buzz us again, Dad!'

He'd turn through the sky, banking away from the white cumulonimbus on the horizon, and come back again, approaching low over us, over the creek and its dead baboon, the guava trees, the tall grass. The hum would deepen until it became a roar; he'd tilt his wings, salute, and with a whoosh he'd be gone.

I stand at the window, watch my father's back, his faded green wellies, his skin weathered and dark from so many years in the sun. And as I watch, I think of him working to stay positive. All these years and I never knew that his is a constant effort. He crouches down, working quickly, happily, scraping leaves and cut branches together with his worn gardening gloves, dropping them in handfuls into the green wheelbarrow. As I watch, it seems the abundant garden grows around him and from him, reaching up to the summer clouds, its new leaves tugging towards the sky.

PART VII:
ENGLAND
2006 Onwards

Me, William and Anna with White Rhino in Meru, Kenya, 1980.

Thirty-Two

18 August 2006

I recognise him the moment he walks in: the glasses with rec-tangular black frames, the reddish curling hair. He walks fast and happily. He moves openly and easefully. He comes straight to where I am sitting with a book on my lap, waiting for him to arrive. I stand up quickly and hug him, so that my companions at the table won't realise we've never met before, and he smiles broadly.

'Caroline? I'm so sorry I'm late,' he begins.

'This is Mike,' I say, turning back to the two men at my table. They tell us their orders, and Mike and I go together to the bar.

'I told them I was waiting for my boyfriend,' I explain. 'Mine was the only table with any space left so they asked if they could join me. Apparently there's a wedding in the village tomorrow, which is why it's so busy. Sorry, but we'll have to pretend to know one another.'

'Great,' he says, beaming at me. 'Then I won't have to ask you if you have any brothers or sisters.'

We've met in an old country pub that neither of us knows, in a village at the top of a hill. I drove up here from my parents' house, where I'm staying for a couple of weeks at the end of the summer until I move into a shared flat with friends in Shepherd's Bush, not far from my work at the BBC. The village where we've met is equidistant between my parents' house in the country and the part of South London where Mike said he was going to be collecting a piece of musical equipment. We'd chosen it arbitrarily on a map as we spoke on the phone to organise our date.

Mike sets down the bottle of red wine for us and the whiskies for our two companions, then we sit together on the cushioned bench that runs under the windows. He puts his arm around me and I laugh.

'How long have you two been together?' asks Mac, the more dominant one. He lives on a boat in Hornsea, up on the Yorkshire coast. Mike was late, stuck in traffic, so I've had time to get to know something about Mac and his friend Ian: they work together repairing boats. Ian is quiet and shy. He's Mac's apprentice in the boat business. They'd pulled chairs up to my table and Mac had talked animatedly.

'Two years,' Mike says, turning to me as though to check. 'Is that right, my love?'

'Wish I had your luck,' Mac says, leaning back in his chair, the pale tip of a tattoo emerging from the collar of his T-shirt along the side of his neck.

I can't quite place Mike, his voice, the way he talks. Mac's companion is leaning in towards the three of us now, more at ease, his hands around his whisky, enjoying himself, and I can see that they like Mike, and that he likes them too. He brims over with enthusiasm and energy. I can see he's one of those people who lift any situation, who can make anyone laugh.

We don't stop talking all evening, switching without much difficulty – thanks to the roar of pre-wedding conversation and laughter going on all around us – between our private conversation and the one we're having with the other two at the table, pretending we've known each other for years. Mike tells me he spent his childhood on a farm in Buckinghamshire, with his parents who were farmers and his two older brothers. The grandparents on both sides were farmers too, and for generations before that. But the boys didn't want to farm – they all wanted to be musicians – so when it was time to retire his parents sold the farm. When he left college he moved to London, but he's spent most of the last fifteen years abroad, working as a musician. He taught himself to play by ear, listening to his brothers' Beatles' records and playing along on a dusty old piano left to them by a great-aunt. He still doesn't read music, he tells me. Then Mac asks us something and we lean forward once more. Mike puts his arm around me and squeezes me, making me laugh again. 'Just playing along,' he says.

The landlady rings the bell for last orders and slowly the customers leave. There's one room left at the pub, room number five, and we take it. We say goodbye to Mac and Ian, and return to the same bench by the windows.

The landlady locks up the pub, then takes her place behind the bar and gets out a bottle for the regulars. A man at a stool near her starts to sing, and from behind the bar the landlady joins in. It's an old folk ballad and they sing it together with an easy familiarity. When they've finished, the landlady clears her throat and begins another.

We sit close to each other, the impromptu performance playing out over the swirly carpet, the old ashtrays and the yellow-shaded candelabras on the walls. We don't have to go anywhere. Neither of us has to be anywhere else until the following morning.

'If nobody's here when you leave in the morning,' says the landlady, 'just post the keys back through the letterbox.' She is wiping the bar, in wide sweeps with an old cloth, and the last of the regulars are taking their leave.

We climb up the creaking stairs behind the bar area. In the small crooked room there's a kettle and next to it two shortcake biscuits in a plastic wrapper on a white tray by the box TV. While Mike is in the bathroom I undress and wrap my long red shawl around myself. I fold my clothes over the back of the chair and climb into the bed. Mike reappears, folds his glasses, places them on the side table by the bed, then climbs in beside me and puts his arms around me. We talk and laugh late into the night, then we sleep this way until the first light comes in through the thin curtains.

'Let's keep the biscuits,' he says. 'Lucky biscuits.'

He puts them in the glove compartment where they will stay for the next three years, until the day we decide to sell the car. That day I'll clear out the car – it's parked on the steep street outside the house we share in North London, near an outdoor pool where I love to swim, and a hill we walk on, and a small, sunny roof terrace crowded with plants bursting out of their pots. And I'll find them there, the lucky biscuits, still in their wrapper, but turned to a fine golden dust.

We drive away from the pub in the quiet of the early morning. The day hasn't yet begun in earnest. I follow Mike's old German car over the crest of the hill, past the church, down the winding hill on the other side and back to the main road. As we drive, the mist begins to rise off the hill, floating up into a blue August sky.

Thirty-Three

Brighton, 2009

I lay my fingertips on the wooden table and look around the room. The builders have left for the day and the house is empty, smelling of dust and plaster, old walls and wooden floorboards uncovered. It smells of age, this house. It was neglected when we bought it – a gentle sort of neglect of its outside, its window frames and walls and roof, though I loved the old man's tattered armchair in the living room, his long narrow office and his serious, peaceful desk at the end of it: the last evidence of the work of a life. In his bedroom each drawer and cupboard was labelled in elderly cursive writing, like my grandmother's: Stockings, Briefs, Socks. The old man's wife had dementia, and it seemed he had taken to labelling things to aid her memory. All of that has gone now, taken away by their children. Part of the roof has come off, a whole floor has been removed, so cables and wires dangle in mid-air. The walls have been stripped back, and what I smell is an old smell of bricks and dust covered over and now released.

The walled garden is now full of rubble, so the grass beneath it has been destroyed, though many of the climbing roses have clung on, wild now, shooting long, strong, thorned branches at odd angles away from the walls. I have asked Mike to make sure that nothing harms the fig tree in the corner, nor the cherry tree growing awkwardly from the middle of this small square garden. In its corner the fig twists and turns over the old garden wall, its branches and lobed leaves reaching high above it, hiding the surrounding townhouses from our view. The fig has probably been there for a hundred years or more, perhaps a hundred and eighty, the age of the house itself.

I was working abroad when Mike first saw the house. He called me from the street outside to tell me he'd found it, the one we were looking for.

I haven't got involved much in the project. Mike is managing it, with his brother, and the two of them together have enough ideas and enthusiasm for everyone. On the wall of what was once the old man's living room they have drawn a diagram floor plan of the house, arrows pointing this way and that, figures scrawled all over it, crossed out, recalculated. Written straight onto the old peeling paint by the kettle is a list of names – Mike's and his brother's as well as all those of the builders on the project – and how they like their tea. The kettle is exhausted, scale-encrusted, covered with dust and fingermarks. There's a small fridge next to it with milk and a packet of biscuits, sometimes the remains of a sandwich, a cream cake. On top of the fridge a box of teabags torn open, a grimy jar of instant coffee, a bag of sugar, tea stains down the white paper bag, everything covered in dust.

I pull out the stool and sit on it, look into the garden. The front of the house at ground level has been knocked down so there's nothing between me and the garden, nothing but ladders, bricks, a bag of plaster, planks laid over a big hole in the ground that leads to the basement.

For reasons I can't explain, I'm having one of those days when nothing clicks into place. Underneath the mild nausea I've been experiencing, a side effect of being four months pregnant, I have a general feeling of unease today. I've been ignoring it, pushing it away, getting on with my day, but now that I am still and alone, in the unfinished house surrounded by the evidence of the others' productive, energetic day, it surfaces. And the old thought comes to me: I know what would take this away, this treacherous feeling, this uncertainty. I haven't done it for months and months, in fact I can't clearly remember the last time, it was a long time before I was pregnant; but nonetheless, it's still there, as an option. I can access it, I can always access it, even if I don't actually do it. I know it's there, should I need it, as back-up.

I think it through in a purely logistical way first. There's a functioning toilet in the house and Mike won't be back for some time. He and his brother have gone to look for old doors at a timber yard. I picture them in the van, windows down, talking fast, plotting and planning, radiating energy wherever they go.

There's a shop near the house, a whole series of shops, just a minute away. It's simple; I could do it. I stand up, pick up my bag, cast around for an empty plastic bag. I don't want to bring any more rubbish back to the house.

I'm going to do it, I decide. I'm not going to challenge it; I'm not going to analyse it, I'm just going to do it. I'll walk out and I won't think about it, I won't think what I am trying to think, which is that I don't want to do it here, in my new home, in a place that is clean, where I have never done it before, where there still lingers on every floor, in every room, the memory of the family who lived here for twenty or thirty or fifty years, the dignified old man and his wife. He always wore a hat, and raised it to neighbours and passers-by on the street. I won't think that; I'll just do it.

It's only minutes before I'm back, with my bag of food.

I unpack the bag. A loaf of white bread, butter, cake, biscuits. I snap the empty plastic bag out, tie it into a loose knot, place it on the table. I rub my lower back, and contemplate the food. I hear a high-pitched machine somewhere, mixed with the other sounds of this city and the sea. Over the wall, over the rubble, through the exposed front of the house, come the sounds of seagulls, traffic, the voices of schoolkids making their way down the street. The sounds of industry and movement and wind.

I look at the bread: it's lopsided. It dips down like a horse's back on top, and flops to one side in its see-through plastic bag. It's all white and shades of white and a very pale brown crust. It's soft. I press onto it with my hand. It doesn't regain its shape so I pick up the bag and shake it gently, reunite the slices, lay it gently back on the table, its slices neatly stacked, side by side. Then I just look at it, all of it, spread over the table.

I feel nothing.

Even if I wanted to, I could not bring myself to eat this, to go through with what I've started. I can't do it. I stare down at the food. I don't know what I'm trying to achieve with the bread, the cake, the packet of biscuits spread before me; I can't think why on earth I would go through with it. I'm trying to reignite something that has died. The great fantasy, the lie, the belief that this was my map through darkness, has finally crumbled away to dust. Those pathways in my brain that associated all this with pleasure, with release, with the powerful but senseless idea that this could help anything at all, have closed down and gone for ever. It's over, and I can't do it, not even this one last time. It's the end of the affair.

I pick my way out into the corner of the garden, where there is still some threadbare grass, to call my mother, to let her know what time we'll be getting back to their house, to ask if there is anything we can pick up for her on our way back, anything she needs. I picture her in the kitchen, apron tied around her, specks of finely chopped parsley on her fingertips. She is cooking a Lebanese dish, she tells me, *sayyadiyeh*, fish with rice, onions, pine nuts, because she knows I like that kind of thing. With a salad of chopped tomato and parsley and spring onion, in a lemon juice and olive oil dressing. She plunges the tomatoes into boiling water for a minute, she says, till their skins just split, so she can peel them, so they are tender and juicy. I remember my grandmother making this same salad, splitting tomato skins, then holding the knife carefully in her bent fingers, chopping the tomatoes as their juice ran off the board.

My mother's voice grounds me. I can't wait to be in her kitchen, with her. I'm filled with relief, with a sharp and clear appreciation of the peace and the possibilities of the moment. The wind from the sea blows over the walls and into the garden where I stand. The smell of it is salty and peaty, of seaweed, the cries of the gulls sharper and more urgent than they were before. I check the time. I have time to swim out into the sea, to the yellow buoys bobbing offshore, before Mike gets back and we close up the house for the night.

It's funny, I don't feel euphoric, not at first, not until my head is under the first waves. Instead, as I assemble the food in the fridge, lock the gate, and head down the street towards the mass of blue and the crests of white, I feel a dissipating weariness, and a dissipating sadness, as though the last chapter of a very long story in which I have been completely engrossed has come to an end, and I can put it down now and walk away.

Thirty-Four

Some years later
At my parents' home in Sussex, 2012

I'd like to know the names of all the trees in my parents' garden, in the part of the countryside they live, and I'd like to teach my two children the names of English trees. I pick up a serrated leaf and hold it up to my mother, who is at the other end of the table sorting through her own mother's old handwritten recipes.

'That's an elm,' she says. 'And the one with the more rounded lobes . . .'

'This one?' I ask, holding up a leaf. 'I know this one, it's from the oak.'

'Yes, that's right.'

I staple the leaf onto the paper and write the name of the tree next to it. Elm, Oak, Chestnut, Birch. At the top I write 'Trees in the Garden' and I stick it to my parents' fridge with magnets.

The children run past the kitchen window, their long canes of leaf-topped bamboo swinging high in the air, followed by my father pushing his wheelbarrow full of leaves. They have been helping him in the garden. I follow their calls and laughter to the other side of the garden and watch them, through the old small-paned windows whose wood is steadily warping and eroding, despite being regularly gouged back and patched up by my father.

As I turn to go back into the kitchen I hear a cry. Our son, who is three, has fallen over on the tarmac of the moss-invaded tennis court. I see my father pick him up and dust him off. He's fine, I can see he hasn't really hurt himself. I watch my father crouch over him, rubbing the grit from his small knee. The two of them are like a big and a small version of each other, with the same thick, dark-brown hair, the same strong, well-proportioned bodies. Our daughter has fine, curling hair, slightly chestnut in colour, like Mike's.

'Be a brave boy now,' I hear my father saying. 'Little boys don't cry.'

George stops his crying, but looks as though he might start again. I'm waiting for the roar. It's what Dad has taken to doing recently if the grandchildren whine. He roars at them like a lion and it usually stops them.

'Come on,' Dad calls out, and the kids chase after him. 'Let's go and look at the horses.'

The three of them disappear around the side of the house.

I check the clock on the kitchen wall.

'I'd better start packing up,' I say to Mum. 'Mike is getting back around six, so we'll aim to arrive home at the same time.'

'Do you have time for tea in the garden before you go?' she asks. 'Nothing special, just a lemon cake from the farm shop.'

I fill the kettle and look in the bread bin for the cake, cut us each a slice while Mum makes the teas.

We walk into the garden with the tray and cross the mossed grass to the bench that is still just within the low sunshine, calling for the children and my father. Dad appears from the end of the garden near the driveway with George on his shoulders, holding Polly by the hand. George is crumpled forward, his small head resting on my father's, his boots spreading mud on the old jumper Dad wears to garden in. Polly is waving a stick like a *panga* – *swish, swish, swish*, she swings at the grass as they walk. George is asleep, his red lips slightly parted.

'I put George on my shoulders because he wanted to be carried, but we were at the horses by the time I realised he'd fallen asleep,' Dad says.

He eases George gently off his shoulders and into his arms, cradling him against his shoulder. Then he carries him into the house and, in the garden's last light from the kitchen windows, he lays him down on the sofa, places a cushion gently beneath his head and tucks a blanket tenderly around him.

The next morning I cycle along the seafront near our home in Brighton. It is a beautiful sea today, all shifting expanses of darker and lighter blue. A clear wind from across the water blows around me, blows past me, and I breathe it in in deep lungfuls. I cycle fast through the wind: the wind, the sea, the sky, my landscape now, the first and second E in DEFOE, Exercise and Environment, lifting me to another plane.

A good day, in a sea of other good days. The urge to lose it is so remote, it's now just a memory, just the odd sighting of that small island of detritus floating out there, far away. It is a freedom I only gradually regained, in fits and starts, over the course of the year during which I saw Penny, and in the subsequent years, until the illness finally disappeared altogether. The tail-end of it was thin but persistent, a bad day here and there in a month or two, enough to feel derailed for a couple of days. But eventually, even that died away.

The summer after Mike and I met, we moved in together to a house in North London. There was an outdoor pool, a lido, near the house, and whenever the old thinking resurfaced I would swim there, up and down, up and down, and I knew that if I did that, I'd be back to myself. There was also a hill we could climb for our 'life-saving walks', as Mike called them. When I felt dragged down, we would walk up to the top of the hill, in winter or summer, day or night, and he would encourage me to talk. It always began the same way, with me marching silently towards the hill, caught up in a struggle I didn't really understand. But before long I would be able to look up, to look around me. I would be able to see what it was that was bothering me, and I would feel the dark mood lifting away like the mist that lifted off the hill our first morning in August. And there he would be, still wearing the scarf I gave him the week we met, its soft edges eaten away by moths.

Sometimes, like anyone else, I still need to work at Being Positive. Mike has to remind me to turn outwards, not inwards like the red anemone. I think of DEFOE, I think of the wildebeest, of my brother's ebbs and flows. Then I'll swim in the sea and feel any heaviness physically trailing away from me, spreading out into the water like sparkling plankton. In winter I'll walk on the beach. I'll walk until I am lifted, high on the wintry landscape.

I cycle home as quickly as I can, standing up on the pedals. I'm back on my chopper bike on my way to the giraffe pond, but I am also here, and the wind blows around me again. Here, the sea, in shifting shades of blue, different bodies of water meeting, like the White and the Blue Niles outside Khartoum which even now, as I cycle alongside this English sea, come together in a flat heat in the desert. And whereas, before, this thought might threaten to topple me, now it is a source of amazement.

Life is not fixed. I know that now. And, like anyone else, I have the power to change its course. I wouldn't wipe out the bad years, even if I could. Because now I am free, and now I understand what it is to be free, in even the simplest of moments.

Every day, even now, there is a moment when I'll look up from what I'm doing, startled by a sudden consciousness of uninterrupted peace.

I open the garden gate, step inside. Our children run to me. I drop to my knees on the grass to hold them. I bury my face in their hair and kiss their soft cheeks. Their heads are as smooth and as silky as that part of a young goat under the neck, where the soft fold of skin hangs down. And, in this moment, there is nothing else, just the grass under my knees and their small heads against me, and a simple, soaring happiness.

Chicken-watching. Kenya, 1981.

Timeline

Nigeria:	1968–1973	*William and Anna born
Ethiopia:	1973–1976	*Caroline born, 1974
Lesotho:	1976–1980	
Kenya:	1980–1985	
Sudan:	1985–1986	
Kenya:	1986–1988	
Pakistan:	1988–1992	
Boarding school:	1991–1993	
Ethiopia:	1992–1996	
Oxford:	1994–1998	
Uganda:	1996–1999	
England:	1999–present	

Acknowledgements

I began to write this book in earnest shortly after the birth of our first child and continued to write it over a number of years, spanning the birth of our second child. So I am thoroughly indebted to the people and places that enabled me to write, even with very small children.

Thanks first and foremost to Mike for supporting me through the ups and downs of writing, for the encouragement, humour and perspective, and for providing me with the space to continue with this project, which I have loved.

Thanks to my parents whose support and dependability have been unfailing throughout, to my sister who read early drafts and whose encouragement kept me going and to my brother who read a proof in Tanzania and returned with understanding, help and energy for the last phase.

Thanks to Farina Pakulat, Laye Dieng, Kicki Ringqvist and Leonardo Guedes, our extended family who have, over time, so beautifully and generously helped to look after our children, and without whom I could never have made progress.

Thanks to the room at the Craftsman where I made early notes, the Jubilee Library in Brighton, my parents' dining room with its old windows, the room at the top of this house with its view of the sea: all peaceful, inspiring places to write.

My greatest thanks to my agent Kerry Glencorse for her unfailing support, encouragement and brilliant editorial input right from the beginning of the project, without which I never would have got anywhere near this point.

Thanks to Andreas Campomar, my excellent editor from Constable for believing in the book and taking it on. Thanks to Claire Chesser from Constable for her expert guidance, advice and help in bringing all the strands together, and to Sue Phillpott for her admirable copyediting talent.

Finally, thank you, Penny Forster, for setting me back on the path to a rich and fulfilled life. I can only hope this book might help others, through the simple recognition of a shared experience.